Basic Guide to the Dalmatian

*Written by breeders
who know the breed...
For those who are interested in
learning more about the
Dalmatian*

Copyright 1997 by Dace Publishing
All rights reserved. This book, or parts thereof,
may not be reproduced in any form without permission.
Published by Dace Publishing
P.O. Box 91, Ruckersville, VA 22968

To all those who have challenged me: "Here's to you......."

Printed in the United States of America

ISBN 0-932045-12-X
Library of Congress Catalog Card Number 96-96109

Front Cover:
CH. COACHMAN'S CUP O' TEA
Owned by Dr. Chris & Phyllis Fetner
Coachman Kennels, Reg ~ Dallas, TX — See Page 65

Back Cover:
CH. COACHMAN'S CAKE WALK
Owned by Jean & Wm. W. Fetner
Coachman Kennels, Reg ~ Rocheport, MO — See Page 65

The *Basic Guide to the Dalmatian* is written from information collected about the breed from some of the top breeders in the nation. In this way the material presented is not only breed specific, but is an overview of the breed as seen by many kennels and breeders, not the breed as viewed by a single individual and limited to his experiences. We would like to thank the following people for their help in putting this project together.

Michael R. Zervas - Managing Editor
Stephen W. Jones - Project Editor
Trevor Shand - Production Coordinator

And a special thank you for the tremendous help we received from the following owners, breeders, handlers and of course, lovers of the Dalmatian.

CONTRIBUTING AUTHORITIES IN NO PARTICULAR ORDER:

Dr. Swift	Dr. Colin Hagan	Leonard & Paula Lisciotto
Cathy & Sam Murphy	Candace Allen	Bob & Gilda Aguilera
Norma & Ray Baley	Janice Brennan	Elaine Dodson
J.R. Jones	Sandra Jankowski	Barbara Kalbach
Paul & Elaine Lindhorst	Dr. Barry Gardner	Patrick & Linda Jones
Alison Aguilera	Al Kay	Christine Nowacki
Carol Curlee	Robert & Diana Skibinski	Kathryn Blink
Paula Miller	Barbara Niemeyer	Carol Shulte
Tina Thomas Smith	Mary Squire	Brad & Peggy Ann Strupp
Jack & Dianna Teeter	Dr. Irvin Krukenkamp	Patricia Wallace-Jones
Susan Geisler	Eva & Kenneth Berg	Carol & Dennis Herbold
Suzanne Stoll	Gary & Joan Smith	Bronwyn Schoelzel
Sherryl Smith	Peter Capell	Jean & Wm W. Fetner
Meg & Mike Hennessey	J. Richard Millaire	Dr. Billie Ingram
Mollie & Billy Jackson	Joanne & Jim Nash	Dr. Chris & Phyllis Fetner
Jena Zafiratos	Dennis & Karen Trout	Sara & John Ledgerwood
Ellen Murray	John Foy	Anne Goldman-Hennigan
Chris Jackson	Julie & Ron Lux	Chicagoland Dalmatian Club
Central Carolina Dalmatian Club		Dalmatian Club of Northern California
Melissa Erikson		

Your years of knowledge and interest in the breed, has not only made this book possible, but it insures the future of the Dalmatian.

Table of Contents

Section I

Introduction..7
History..9
    Where the breed originated and what were its purposes.
Should You Buy a Dalmatian?.................................17
    Living with a Dalmatian, fitting the dog to your lifestyle.
The Standard..24
    What a Dalmatian should look like.
Finding a Breeder..30
    How to look for a breeder, what questions to ask, what to expect from a breeder, what not to expect.
Health..44
    Health problems frequent in the breed and how to view them.
Bringing Home a New Dog or Puppy.....................52
    What to expect when you bring home a new family addition, and how to be prepared so everyone gets off to a good start.
The Paperwork..58
    Registration papers, pedigree information.
Dog Shows and Other Competitions......................62
    Dog Shows and Obedience Trials, Road Trials and more.
Care..105
    Daily care, normal veterinarian care, what to feed, daily exercise, type of environment needed.
Training..109
    Socialization, puppy training, obedience.
Shipping and Travel..114
    Shipping, traveling with your dogs, what to do when your dog stays home.
Breeding Your Dog — Why this may not be such a good idea!..........................117
    A realistic view of breeding your dog.

Section II

Hall of Fame..64
    A photo gallery of some outstanding examples of the breed.
Shopping Arcade...124
    Where to find some interesting and unusual products related to the Dalmatian.

HOW TO USE THE BASIC GUIDE BREED SERIES

This series of books is written for the person who is investigating the breed for a possible pet; for the person who has decided on a Dalmatian and wants to know how to find a good breeder and what to ask; for the person who has just bought a Dalmatian who wants to know what to expect and how to train it; and for the person who owns a Dalmatian who wants to know more about the breed and how closely his or her dog resembles current champions and outstanding dogs of the breed. These books are also a *beginning point* for those who want to know what else they can do with their dogs.

The Basic Guide to the Dalmatian takes a unique approach. Instead of being the opinion of one kennel, with one style of dog and one view of the breed, we have interviewed many breeders and have pooled their vast knowledge and interest in the breed to create an overview as **NO OTHER BREED BOOK** provides. The knowledge and experience reflected here are not limited to a single person.

This series is truly educational for the reader. In many places, where breeders have given us conflicting information, we have pooled that information, making note that there is a dispute within the breed and indicating that further discussion with individual breeders is advisable.

OUR TWO SPECIAL SECTIONS

The **HALL OF FAME** section not only puts new people in contact with breeders of top quality animals as a place to start their search, but it also gives the reader a chance to see the different styles within the breed. By carefully studying the pedigrees provided, it is a start in understanding the relation of the pedigree to the individual dog - the cornerstone upon which breeds and breed registries are built. If you already own a Dalmatian, you might enjoy looking through this section and comparing your dog and its pedigree with those who have been achievers in the world of dogs!

Finally, the **SHOPPING ARCADE** section puts readers in contact with some of the fine businesses whose products relate to dogs and to Dalmatians in particular. For those of us who show dogs on a regular basis, we meet some of these fine specialty businesses every week. For those who do not attend such events, the Shopping Arcade section provides a chance to find these quality products which will make excellent gifts for the breed lover, additions to your home, or products to help you raise a happy, healthy dog.

We sincerely hope you find this book informative and entertaining and that you have as much fun reading it as we have had producing it, and as much fun as our breeders have had producing fine quality dogs for so many years.

BEFORE YOU BUY A DOG

1) Decide WHAT YOU WANT THE DOG TO DO. Evaluate your home and lifestyle and how a dog should fit into your life.

2) Look at different breeds and decide what breed is best for you and your home.

3) Realize that there are differences in style and temperament within each breed. Different breeders select their breeding stock based on different criteria. Use the Hall of Fame to help you see the differences among dogs and kennels.

4) Find a breeder who produces dogs which will fit your needs. Ask questions which will insure that the dog you buy will be right for you by finding a breeder who places importance on the qualities which are important to you.

5) Be sure to ask the breeder the right questions for that particular breed and be prepared for what the breeder will want to ask you.

With this in mind, your decision will be an informed one and the dog you buy will be a welcome addition to your family for years to come.

The Dalmatian has long been regarded as the "Fire Dog." Originally he was a coach dog and his love of horses led him to the fire house with its teams of heavy working horses which drew the early fire wagons in the growing cities. He ran ahead, his sharp bark warning the crowds of the charging fire wagon and thundering horses. When motorized fire trucks replaced the horse drawn vehicles, the Dalmatian made the change. Today he is still a symbol of firefighters. Above is **Jaybar's Sprinkles,** and John Foy at the Ventura, California Fire Department where "Joy" has her own badge!

INTRODUCTION

We are often asked, "Why buy a purebred dog?" Certainly there are some wonderful, loving and even talented mutts. But have you ever owned a dog, or known a mutt you admired and been frustrated in trying to locate another like him?

Centuries ago, people kept dogs for pets, for working partners in their fields and with their flocks, as hunting companions, and for protection of the family. As dogs began to diversify, people noticed certain dogs were better at one thing than others. People liked the looks of one dog over another, or found that one had better instincts in certain areas than another. Dogs in one geographic area began to look alike from interbreeding within a small population, and people who lived in other areas came to buy such dogs when they wanted a certain characteristic or look. Thus dog breeds began to evolve. The breeds were based on predictability of looks and performance in a dog from a certain area or gene pool.

Breeders, and later field or kennel clubs began to keep records of individuals. This recording of the gene pool is a second step in creating a breed. Without such record keeping, a breed will change and lose characteristics. Again, it is insurance that a puppy will grow to look and act like certain other individuals.

Finally, people wrote descriptions of the breed. At first these were simply descriptions of certain dogs which impressed the author on a hunt, or in traveling. These descriptions are our earliest written standards. Later, breeders banded together to form breed clubs and they wrote a detailed, collective description of the breed for others to follow. Careful breeders who studied the standard, thought about the original purpose of the breed, and were concerned about health and temperament, continued the breed.

The value of a breed, and a registration to record it, is that a buyer of a puppy can predict what it will look like when it is grown up, what its talents and temperament will be and how well it will fit a living situation. If we owned and raised nothing but crossbreeds, or if you simply got a cute puppy from the dog pound, you would have no way of knowing what you might be sharing your home and your life with for the next twelve to fourteen years!

And there is a certain pride of ownership in a stylish, quality dog. It does not take an experienced eye to tell the difference between a fine antique and a fake, between a fine luxury car and a clunker. To say that there is no reason to get a purebred dog instead of a mutt is like saying that a Geo will get you there just as well as a Cadillac. Both fill the same job of taking the driver from one place to another, but the pride of ownership is entirely different. It does not take training to recognize quality in an animal. It is manifested in the way the dog comes together, the way the over-all animal pleases the eye, the attitude and presence — the self confidence — of the dog. Good breeding, soundness, and aptitude of purpose are a source of pleasure. If you divide the cost of the average puppy from a good breeder, by the life span of the dog, you will be paying less than fifty dollars a year, or about four dollars a month for the pleasure of an animal that will be recognizable as his breed, serve the purpose for which he was bred, and have the health and temperament that will make him fit your family and life-style.

Dalmatians can do a lot of different things. This puppy has grown up and is now serving as a hearing dog for a deaf Vietnam Veteran.

In this way, you will find an animal that will be a good fit, one that will share your home and your love for a lifetime, instead of getting a puppy that grows into an individual you cannot live with, and one which causes frustration and stress.

Breeders find that new owners who take this kind of time to locate a puppy are far more likely to be satisfied with their new family member. They are more likely to realize what care of that breed will entail, will be more likely to provide a good home, and far less likely to take it to the pound or otherwise get rid of the animal.

So, take the time to do your homework about the breed. A dog is not only what it looks like, but how easy it is to live with in a given situation. No breed is perfect for everyone. Find out what questions to ask for that particular breed, locate breeders, and take your time to find a puppy or adult dog which will meet your needs. For those purposes, we hope these <u>BASIC GUIDE</u> books will be helpful.

HISTORY

*L*ike many breeds, the history of the Dalmatian is obscure and difficult to document. One thing is for certain. The breed is spelled DalmatiAn, *not* DalmatiOn. This common misspelling will be sure to irritate the Dalmatian breeder. Before you begin to seriously consider owning a breed, it is reasonable to expect that you will at least learn the correct name for the breed.

There is no evidence that they came from Dalmatia, an area which lies along the coast of what was once Yugoslavia, and is currently under the control of Croatia, although part of it, including the old city of Dubrovnik, is sometimes claimed by Bosnia Herzegovina. Dalmatia lies along the Adriatic Sea, just across from Italy, and was part of the old trade routes of antiquity. There are no Dalmatians in Dalmatia today, and no evidence that there ever have been, except for a period after 1930, when Mr. Bozo Banac, a wealthy English shipowner, imported them from England to his home near Dubrovnik, where they were known locally as "the English Dogs." By 1954 — it was reported — the last remaining dog

of this imported stock was in Dubrovnik, the line presumably having died out with this animal. Later, English breeding stock was imported and used by several serious breeders in Zagreb and Zupanja, located in Northern Croatia, but no one seems to know if their work, largely done in the 1970s, has been continued. Certainly with the political unrest in the area within the last decade, no new importation or breeding has occurred.

Why the breed is called Dalmatian is not known. If they did not originate in that area, how the name came to be linked with the breed is not recorded. There are various other explanations, none of which has any substantial basis in recorded history. One popular theory is that the dogs took their name from a white ecclesiastical garment called a dalmatic. Many of them can be seen in the Vatican Museums. Dating back to early Christian times, these ecclesiastical garments were originally made of soft wool. Throughout the history of the church, these vestments became more ornate and finally, some came to be trimmed in ermine. It is possible that the ermine trim reminded people of the markings of the dogs.

Although the tunic-like dalmatic was worn by popes, bishops and even monarchs during their coronations, a simple version was worn by the Dominican Order of Friars. These habits included the dalmatic and a black gown worn over it. The black and white of the garment is like that of the dog, and is considered to be a reference to a fresco in Florence in the Capella della Spagnoli (Spanish Chapel) of Santa Maria Novella. This allegorical work portrays lambs being set upon by a wolf. One lamb is in the wolf's jaws, another is fleeing, and spotted dogs, which look like Dalmatians, are ferociously attacking the wolf. If the priests are portrayed by the dogs, saving their flock of parishioners, the coat color of the dogs is associated with the dalmatic, and the connection is made for the name of the breed.

Further support of this theory comes from the Inquisition, when the Dalmatian was frequently used by the Dominicans as an allegorical representation of their order. This connection was so strong that during the Cromwell years in England (1649-1660) the spotted dog was used in antipapal leaflets as a symbol of the Roman rule of the Catholic church in England. The British Museum houses political woodcuts of that period which include dogs which look like Dalmatians in build and coloring.

Although dogs have been companions and working partners of man from prehistoric times, dog breeding and registries which record the lineage of dogs are a fairly recent phenomenon. Ancient people had no dog shows, and their only consideration was if the dog could do the job it was required to do. "Breeds" were localized, resulting from similar ancestors being crossed within a fairly small geographic area, and sometimes traveling along trade routes to other parts of the world. There they would again localize, often resulting in a breed which, within a few generations, looked very different than the original ancestors. Because no one made an effort to keep a breed pure, new dogs entering the area were crossed with local dogs in the hopes of further improving the qualities needed in the work at hand.

In the case of the Dalmatian it was not so much distinguished by its work as the general sleek appearance and its remarkable markings. As unique as the Zebra's stripes, the Dalmatian's unusual spotting pattern is alone in the canine world. We trace the early history of the breed, as we do with many breeds of antiquity, through early prints and drawings which depict animals of like qualities as those we see in the modern breed. Although all dogs go back to a common ancestry, breed origins are traced through common and distinctive traits shared over centuries, and sometimes millennia, and substantiated by what can be found in folklore.

The first drawing of a dog which looks like the modern Dalmatian is a print which clearly shows a dog of Dalmatian type, with excellent spotting, running alongside an ancient war chariot, probably dating back to Egypt or Babylon. The royal tombs of Egypt show spotted dogs. From drawings and frescos of the period of the Inquisition, we know that the spotted dogs existed in Italy during the early part of this millennium. Mention of the dogs in India, all around the Mediterranean, and into Europe, along with paintings showing them with their famous masters, lead enthusiasts to believe they probably were originally hunting dogs, and much favored by royalty. They have also been connected with the Turks, the Bengals, and the wide ranging Gypsy groups.

Most early written references mention only spotted dogs, and do not describe the spotting. It is unclear if they meant to describe the small, numerous spots of the Dalmatian or the large spots seen in several breeds from the Newfoundland and Great Dane to the Pointer. Even early pictures are sometimes unclear. It is sometimes difficult to discern whether they depict spotting as would be seen in the Dalmatian or simply ticking (only a few

The distinctive spotting of the Dalmatian is unlike any other breed of dog and sets it apart just as the stripes of a Zebra set it apart from any other animal.

scattered hairs in a place) as would be seen in an English Setter. Many of these early pictures include at least one or two large, solid spots on the dog's body.

One of the earliest paintings to include a true Dalmatian was painted by Gerard ter Borch, a famous Dutch painter. It is *The Congress of Munster, 1647* which shows the scene from the Peace of Westphalia which ended the Thirty Years War. The Dauphin of France is accompanied by a dog which looks similar to a Dalmatian and most breeders accept that as evidence that the breed was established by that time.

The Dalmatian began to evolve into the breed he is today after he arrived in England from India during the period of colonization of that country. The first English painting to include a Dalmatian was done by the famous animal artist, James Seymour (1702-1752).

From the early sixteenth century onward, a number of paintings throughout Europe show dogs with the distinctive Dalmatian spotting pattern.

An Italian painting, *Hunting Dogs and their Attendants,* by Francesco Castiglioni, c. 1776, shows heavy dogs with Dalmatian markings. And in a lovely old castle in Berchtesgaden, owned for many years by the Wittelsbachs, the Bavarian Royal House, there is a magnificent cabinet with inlay of ebony and ivory. Heinrich Wahl crafted the inlay during the years he was a political prisoner. The scene was a representation of *Legend of St. Hubert,* finished in 1750, showing two dogs with Dalmatian spotting.

Clifford Hubbard in his *Dogs in Britain* (1948) said, "...[1665] evidence appear(s) of it (Dalmatian) being used in its now traditional role of coach-dog. By 1670 it was certainly used in France as an accessory to travel by coach, and was invaluable as a guard against highwaymen." The endurance of the Dalmatian became important. Coaches in those days were likely to travel fifty to one hundred miles a day, depending on road conditions and weather. The horses were changed at the midpoint of the journey, but the dogs trotted the entire way. Today the Dalmatian is still an endurance dog.

The first written mention of the dog appears in a book called *Natural History,* published in 1790 by the famous French naturalist George Louis Leclerc, Comte de Buffon. He refers to the breed as "Le Braque de Bengale" (Harrier of Bengal).

Thomas Bewick published *History of Quadrupeds*, in Newcastle-on-Tyne in 1791 which included several wood-engravings of Dalmatians. A passage on the breed says, "The Dalmatian, or coach dog has been erroneously called the Danish Dog, and, by Mr. Buffon, the Harrier of Bengal; but for what reason it is difficult to ascertain, as its incapacity for scenting is sufficient to destroy all affinity to any dog employed in pursuit of the hare.

"It is very common in this country at present; and is frequently kept in genteel houses, as an elegant attendant on a carriage. We do not, however, admire the cruel practice of depriving the poor animal of its ears in order to increase its beauty; a practice so general that we do not remember to have seen one of these dogs unmutilated in this way."

But an earlier (c. 1770) painting by John Collet, called *Kitty Coaxer driving Lord Dupe towards Rotten Row,* shows a dog very much like a modern Dalmatian, with uncropped ears.

We know that the Dalmatian found his way to America with the English colonists and rapidly became a symbol of wealth and fashion. Not surprisingly, he was most popular early on with the southern plantation owners who had transplanted the lifestyle of the English aristocracy, complete with coach dogs to ornament their rigs. George Augustine Washington wrote a letter to his nephew, George Washington, on August 12, 1787 in which he discusses a coach dog. George Washington's account books, on exhibit in the Alderman Library at the University of Virginia, note the purchase of a coach dog on August 14, 1787 for the price of 15 shillings.

Today, the Dalmatian still loves to follow horses. He has tremendous endurance and enjoys the journey.

Throughout the nineteenth century, the Dalmatian seemed to be a fascination to the public. He was widely used in England as a fashionable coach dog and his fondness for horses made him a companion of riders of all ages. Several works depict the Dalmatian following children on ponies, in fields with horses, curled up in stables, and of course under the front wheels of genteel carriages. They were stable dogs, not companions of their owners or faithful hunting dogs. One nineteenth century book by W. Taplin, *The Sportsman's Cabinet* (1803), described the breed as "...of no value except to contribute to the splendor of the stable establishment."

Writers again and again speculated on his origin. He was referred to as the English Coach Dog, the Dalmatian and the Danish Dog. Some purported that since he was a favorite of Gypsies, it was only natural that the breed had spread throughout Europe, Eastern Europe, India and as far away into Asia as Tibet. Some distinguish him from the Danish Dog in size, leading many to believe that, while the smaller dog was the Dalmatian, the larger "Danish Dog" became the harlequin Great Dane. There is little similarity between the breeds, however, except for the fact that both are black and white spotted dogs. There is no similarity in the *type* of spotting, one being large spots like a pinto horse, while the Dalmatian exhibits small spots in great numbers. One interesting note is that mismarked harlequin Great Danes will occasionally have Dalmatian-like spots, while mismarked Dalmatians will sometimes have large, Great Dane-like spots.

Early writings sometimes referred to the dog as being dull or even dim witted. Modern breeders speculate that the characteristic deafness, which has been reduced by selective breeding within this century, was probably very prevalent in the days when deafness in dogs was not recognized and identified. A deaf dog would surely appear to be simply slow-witted, and would be of little use in the field, where he could not respond to calls or whistles of his master or the sounds of the chase. It is no wonder that the prejudice against the Dalmatian built up, and was repeated from writer to writer in regard to its intelligence and working ability. Many of the dog writers of the day, working in the emerging field of identifying and categorizing different breeds — something which was not done until the nineteen century — had no first hand knowledge of the breeds they described, but worked strictly from repeated accounts compiled in other books.

The Dalmatian was beginning to emerge as a useful element in men's lives by the end of the nineteenth century. Major T.J. Woodcock wrote an article in 1891 which stated, "A good Coach Dog has often saved his owner much valuable property by watching the carriage. It is a trick of thieves who work in pairs for one to engage the coachman in conversation while the other sneaks around in the rear and steals whatever robes and other valuables he can lay his hands on. I never lost an article while the dogs were in charge, but was continually losing when the coachman was in charge."

The Dalmatian continued to be in evidence in the United States throughout the nineteenth century. Alistair Cooke's famous work, *America*, has a reproduction of an old stereograph photo of slaves in a Georgia cotton field some time before the Civil War. Almost hidden in the foreground is a dog which is clearly a Dalmatian, lying peacefully on the ground at the feet of the children.

With the growth of cities and the development of regular fire departments, the Dalmatian made the transition from one type of "carriage" to another. Between 1870 and 1910, when the horse drawn firewagon was phased out by Henry Ford's automotive engine, the Dalmatian became a regular inhabitant around the firehouse. His natural ease with and love of horses meant that he was happy to live in the stables of the firehouses, among the horses which pulled the big rigs. He not only was an ornamentation and companion to the firemen, he served the useful purpose of running ahead of the speeding fire wagon, barking loudly and clearing the way. The Dalmatian was the original "siren" for the fire department. He became popularly referred to as "the Fire House Dog."

Dog shows, as we know them today were not known. It was difficult, therefore, for writers and other dog enthusiasts to gain firsthand knowledge of different breeds, and to compare their qualities and distinctions. The first show, held in Birmingham in 1860, represented most breeds of the day, although the distinctions between breeds were very different in many cases from those we recognize today. Dalmatians were exhibited at that show.

By 1872, J.H. Walsh listed the Dalmatian in *Dogs of the British Islands*, in a group

The Dalmatian made the perfect fire house dog because he loved horses, was adapted to living in a stable and because his enthusiasm for his work and sharp bark made him a perfect siren to clear the crowded streets for the approaching fire wagons.

of breeds under the heading "Companionable Dogs." Most of the breeds listed under this heading are today part of the Non-sporting Group in AKC. (See the chapter on dog shows and other competitions.) This marked the first time that Dalmatians had been removed from the category of hounds, field dogs, or gundogs, where they had originally been included.

The British Kennel Club was founded in 1873 to bring order into the rapidly developing dog world. Dog shows were emerging as a sport, and kennel records were kept by some of the large kennels. The first Dalmatian club in England was founded in 1890.

The first group of American breeders organized in 1904, formed a club in 1905 and joined with AKC shortly thereafter. The first Dalmatian to be registered in AKC was "Bessie" who appeared in the fifth volume of the AKC Stud Books. She was recorded as white, black and tan (no longer an acceptable color) with breeder and pedigree unknown. She was whelped in 1887, owned by Mrs. N.L. Havey of San Francisco and apparently produced one offspring. The first AKC Champion Dalmatian was Ch. Edgecomb D'Artagnan, owned by Miss M.W. Martin of Philadelphia, Pa. Bred by J.S. Price, Jr., he was whelped in June 9, 1902 and was black and white. He finished his championship in 1904.

The most active club was in New York and although the Dalmatian Club of America (DCA) was considered a national club, in actuality it was limited to the eastern seaboard. The first specialty show (one held for Dalmatians only) was held in 1926. At least two road trials were held at that time for coaching Dalmatians. They were discontinued for some years, though the instinct for the sport continues in most of the dogs. Recently road trials have been revived, although altered to some extent. Today's road trials include a twelve to twenty-five-mile course held with a horse and rider rather than a coach and test the endurance and suitability of the dog's temperament for work with horses.

Today's Road Trials do not use a carriage. They are a combination endurance test, obedience trial and determination of the dog's compatibility with horses. The Road Trial is a competition unique to Dalmatians and only Dalmatians may earn a Road Trial title. Some of the dogs in our Hall of Fame have Road Trial titles.

The advent of the automobile at the turn of the century reduced the number of Dalmatians in England. World War I saw the interruption of registration in England between 1917 and 1920. Food rationing and the pressure to reduce the number of dogs contributed to the rapid decline of the Dalmatian in England. The Kennel Club show of 1920 had only one Dalmatian entered, and many spectators believed it was the sole survivor of a dying breed. The Dalmatian, however, held on to his foothold in dogdom, and regained popularity so rapidly that by 1930, a Specialty show was held with 458 entries! The names of unregistered animals, whelped during the time of suspended registration, can still be found in extended pedigrees of English Dalmatians.

No such interruption occurred in this country. The original group of twenty-six members of the DCA grew, steadily if not rapidly. Originally limiting membership to fifty, the rules were changed in 1937 because of the growing interest in the breed. The enduring dedication of members to the breed is best exemplified by secretary-treasurer, Miss Flora McDonald, who was elected to the position in 1915 and continued to hold the post until her death in 1967.

When Obedience competition was introduced in the late thirties, Dalmatians were ready for the challenge. The first CD titled Dal was Meeker's Barbara Worth, while Io, owned by Harland Meistrell, was the first CDX, UD and TD Dalmatian. Dalmatians have continued to succeed in obedience, and later in agility.

The famous playwright Eugene O'Neil owned a Dalmatian, "Blemie," with his third wife, actress Carlotta Monterey. O'Neil wrote the "Last Will and Testament of an Extremely Distinguished Dog" when Blemie passed away from old age, and it has survived as a testimony to the love between owners and their Dalmatians.

The book *One Hundred and One Dalmatians,* by Dodie Smith, (1956) boosted the popularity of the breed. The Walt Disney cartoon movie released in 1961 brought the Dalmatian popularity to a new high. With each successive re-release of that movie, Dalmatian breeders report they are overwhelmed by people who are attracted to the darling cartoon figures and children who want a puppy. But not all of these people will make good homes for the breed, and the new Disney version using live Dalmatians may again increase the demand for the Dalmatian as a pet. While this live action movie certainly gives a better representation of what the Dal is really like, many breeders objected to the use of so many young puppies and fear it will cause a number of people to purchase Dalmatians on a whim.

The Dalmatian has become a popular favorite and is frequently seen in commercials and on cards and calendars. Sparky, a Dalmatian who wears a fireman's hat, is a common character used to promote fire safety. Often the symbol of fire prevention week, the Dalmatian is well known to school children all over the country. A Dalmatian accompanies each of several different teams of the famous Budweiser Clydesdales when they perform at special events, in parades and at theme parks all over the country. The Dalmatian is as much a part of the smart look as the polished leather harnesses or the flawlessly groomed horses.

DALMATIANS AROUND THE WORLD

As noted, the Dalmatian was found throughout Europe, where he may have been taken by traveling Gypsy bands. He was found in India and brought to England, which embraced him, and was bred in Italy to the point where he became associated with the Catholic church. Germany and France bred them for hundreds of years. But it was the English who truly molded the breed, began to set a type and improve the stock. The British bloodlines were later used to improve the breed throughout the world.

Today, Dalmatians are found the world over. They are shown in the United States, Canada and throughout the British Commonwealth. They are recognized by the F.C.I. (Federacion Cynologique Internationale), founded in 1911 which regulates shows in over fifty member nations in Europe, Latin America, the Caribbean, Africa, Asia, Australia and New Zealand.

South Africa formed its breed club in 1961 and has produced and shown some very fine dogs. Dog breeding and showing has been a tradition in that country, which has survived political turmoil and managed to produce top international winners in many breeds. Their Dalmatian Specialties in the past have invited both British and American judges who have been pleased with the quality of the dogs they judged.

Dalmatians are very popular in Sweden, where the national club was founded in 1962. From early beginnings at the turn of the century, with dogs principally from Germany, the breed failed to gain a foothold. Then in the early thirties, two dogs were imported from England. These were followed by more English import stock and, later, bloodlines were brought from America. Today, Sweden boasts some fine, well-marked, sound International Champions, and the breed ranks as one of the most popular in the country and throughout Scandinavia.

Luxembourg is a very small country with a large interest in Dalmatians. Its large and active group of enthusiasts work to promote Dalmatians all over Europe. They produce a monthly newsletter which is sent out to many different countries.

Dalmatians in Mexico got off to a slow start. One of the early kennels which produced some very fine dogs was owned by Dr. Phillip Chancellor and called Dalmex. When AKC declared one of his dogs ineligible after it had won an all-breed Best in Show in the United States, he became disenchanted with the breed and disbanded his kennel. Dalmatians have been bred by Manuel Avila Camacho, president of Mexico from 1940-1946, by Ministers of Finance and by several of the wealthy families of that country. Today, largely influenced by American lines, the breed is steadily gaining popularity and building in quality.

Although there are not a large number of breeders in Canada, they are spread out all across the country and have produced some top winning dogs who have shown successfully in both the United States and Canada. The Hall of Fame section features some Canadian breeders. Many of the American kennels and the Canadian kennels are well known to each other and often work together.

SHOULD YOU BUY A DALMATIAN?

*B*efore you buy a dog, any dog, you should ask yourself a few questions. Do you have time for a dog? A dog needs time to be with his human or he will become wild and overexcited when he sees you. He needs time to get exercise, time to be socialized and time to be loved. He needs training and that takes time and consistent patience. He needs regular care. There is expense also with a dog. Yearly shots, bowls, toys and beds are a few of the extras above the cost of feeding him. If you have a family, does everyone in the family want a dog? Who will take care of him, feed him, bathe him and exercise him?

Why do you want a dog? For a companion, to go jogging with you, to sleep at your feet, to greet you when you come home, to protect your home? It is important to identify the role you wish the dog to play before you begin to look for a dog, and even before you decide on a breed. Not every breed is suitable for every home. If you have evaluated your needs, you will be able to find a breed which fits. For example, if you have a lovely home filled with one or two quiet individuals and costly furnishings or antiques, you may not want a Dalmatian. They are active and love to play and may damage a valuable piece simply by knocking it off the table with an excited tail! A Chinese Shar-Pei, a breed which is much more passive, would be a better choice. But if you want a jogging companion, the endurance of a Dalmatian makes him a much better choice than a Shar-Pei, who considers a walk to the food bowl the outing for the day!

Consider that a dog is a long term project. A Dalmatian will live twelve to fourteen years. That is 17% of the average human life-span, more than twice as long as the average television lasts. Not only will the top-of-the-line computer you buy today be gone long before the dog, with the rapid advance of technology, in fourteen years no one will even be able to remember how it worked! If you got married and bought a dog on the same day, statistically speaking, the dog would be more likely to still be with you in a dozen years! It only makes good sense to spend time and energy selecting the right dog.

Once you have decided that you do want a dog and have a clear idea of what you want the dog to do in your home and where he will fit in your life, look at the breeds which appeal to you and see if they match your needs. More than just what breed is close at hand, or what is eye catching to you, see if the characteristics of the breed fit your life. What may be a disadvantage to someone else may be an advantage to you.

Find out what the breed is like from talking to several breeders. Ask about factors which are important to you and your situation. Each year, hundreds and thousands of lovely, purebred dogs end up at the SPCA, and people who have invested money in a good dog are discouraged to find that the pet they dreamed would become a part of their lives for years to come, has become a nightmare. Not EVERY dog in the breed will be the same and not EVERY home is the same. What will fit for one family will be a disaster in another. People have different life patterns and different lifestyles, not to mention differences in homes, yards and time commitments. And people are attracted to different personalities in dogs. What may be fun and appealing to one person may be tiresome and destructive to another. It is important that you begin the process of looking for a dog by carefully evaluating what you want the dog to do, how you want it to behave, and how you want it to live.

Consider, for example, the shedding problem. One breeder says "Dals shed 24 hours a day, 365 days a year — enough said!" Another says, "Dals shed only two times a year — morning and night!" You get the idea. But the problem can be alleviated by regular grooming with a rubber curry. Medical science has proven that stroking or petting a dog substantially reduces stress in people, so grooming can prove to be a mutually beneficial experience. It is not as complicated as the grooming on a long haired dog such as a Cocker Spaniel, and for those who like to play with mechanical toys, a vacuum works well, (though we aren't sure if it has the same properties of stress relief!). But if someone in the family is allergic to dogs, the shedding and high dander will make the Dalmatian almost intolerable. Even with brushing, there will be some shedding. The hair sticks to fabric and is difficult to get up. It is white and shows up on dark clothing so that it is almost impossible to walk out of the house without dog hair on dark pants. One breeder says she invites prospective new owners into her home and waits to see if they begin to obsessively pick the dog hair off their clothing. If they do, she advises them that a Dalmatian is not a good choice for them. But Dalmatians do not have a "doggie" odor, they don't drool, and the coat generally sheds dirt (sometimes on the floor or bedding), keeping them clean and white even without frequent baths.

Most breeders will tell you that their breed is the best. If they didn't think so, they would be putting their time and energy into a different breed. Sometimes dog breeders raise or show several breeds before settling on the one to which they will dedicate their lives and fortunes! Different breeds have the TENDENCY toward certain characteristics based on their history, temperament, size and physical limitations or attributes. Carefully evaluate your home and the tendencies of the breed to determine whether there will be compatibility.

Most dogs who end up in the SPCA are there not because they are BAD dogs, but because they did not fit their homes. Think about it as if you wanted a sports car but had five children to carry around! It wouldn't be very long before the sports car was up for sale, not because sports cars are not fun or because it did not perform well, but because it simply could not do the job that the family with five children needed it to do. It did not fit the situation or the home of the driver.

Another reason dogs end up in the SPCA is that their owners have underestimated the time it takes to socialize and train a puppy. Active breeds with an enthusiastic outlook on life need exercise and training. Without those two things, the dog will be excitable and uncontrollable. Training sessions do not have to be long, but they need to be frequent and consistent. Be sure you have the time to devote and a place for exercise before you buy a Dalmatian.

A Dalmatian is intelligent, playful and intensely loyal. They have been used in circus acts, as guard dogs, war dogs, leader dogs, hearing dogs for the deaf, hunting companions, tracking and rescue dogs and they compete well as obedience and agility dogs. They are usually cool toward strangers, warm and loving to their families and quick at learning new things and adapting to new situations. They will bond to an owner quickly and must be given quality time. This is **not** a dog that is going to go lie in the corner and you will never know it's there.

Dalmatians will weigh about fifty to sixty-five pounds and stand nineteen to twenty-four inches tall when full grown. This makes them about

This Dalmatian is an Assistance Dog and knows 74 commands which makes the life of his master, Melissa Erikson, much easier.

knee high to an adult person. Generally males are larger than females, but individuals may differ. They are "boisterous" and have a sense of humor. If you live a rigid life and expect exact and predictable behavior from a pet, don't buy a Dalmatian. They are clowns, and their inventive imagination leads them to try tricks and games whenever they have the opportunity.

Single career people will be happy with a Dal if they are willing to devote the time to training and are willing to take the dog to places where it can exercise if they live in an apartment. If a person lives in an apartment or other rented abode however, it is necessary to consider if a dog the size of a Dalmatian is acceptable to the landlord and roommates if any. And, if there is a need to change apartments or roommates, how hard will it be to find another place or people who will accept the dog.

Families with children under the age of three should be aware that, as one breeder put it, "either the puppy is too much for the child, the child is too much for the puppy, or they are both too much for the mother!" A well mannered adult dog might be a good alternative. Breeders frequently keep some very promising young dogs and raise them until show age, sometimes even until they finish their championship. Perhaps they are hoping that a dog with potential will turn out to be the show stopper every show breeder is looking for; perhaps they want to see how a certain breeding has turned out. Sometimes they will keep littermates until they are old enough to see which one will be better. Or perhaps they want to show a dog to finish the championship for the kennel, but don't have room to keep the dog after it is finished. In any case, a show breeder will sometimes have a well mannered, well socialized animal which is looking for a nice home. He may have passed the puppy stage, be leash trained and crate trained and, if he has been shown at all, good at taking noise, commotion and people in their stride.

A well-mannered adult Dalmatian makes a good companion, even for a small child, but a puppy may be too much.

Temperament is very important. Dalmatians should not be shy or aggressive. The popularity which has been brought on by the fame the Dal has found in movies and TV has led to a lot of poor breeding. Today, unfortunately, nervous or aggressive temperaments are all too frequent unless you are buying from a good, reputable breeder. Temperament, intelligence and obedience potential go into making a wonderful house companion and are as inherited as size, spotting and structure. Basic puppy socialization by someone who knows how to temperament test and evaluate puppies is an additional factor which ensures that the puppy you get from a reputable breeder will not only be a lovely representation of the breed, but will be a good dog of sound temperament and easy to live with. Dalmatians should **never** be people aggressive.

Living with a Dal is not always easy. He is happy, outgoing and active. He loves to play. A Dalmatian will bring you his ball and want you to throw it for him for hours on end, until you tell him that's enough. They are clowns and do very funny things, and are extremely entertaining. If you don't have time to play, they will invent games on their own. Many a Dalmatian is known to take the ball upstairs and drop it down so he can chase it. They may find the toilet paper and unroll it, or pull pop-up tissues out of the box until it is empty, leaving a heap of tissues they can run through! If you are looking for a quiet dog who never gets into trouble, and constantly tries to please its owner, the Dal is **not** for you.

The "dreadful" puppy stage will last until around three years of age. When the dog finally matures and settles down, he will be a product of the time, energy and consistent patience you have put into him during those trying years. Living with a young Dalmatian resembles living with a lively two-or three-year old and requires full family involvement. It is a challenge to stay one step ahead in the training process, and consistent, firm discipline is necessary.

A bored Dalmatian, left outside, will quickly devise his own methods to amuse himself, sometimes in ways which do not improve the quality of the landscaping or patio furniture. According to our breeders, they can be "stubborn, aggravating and pushy." Like all smart breeds, obedience training is a must unless you are very experienced with large dogs. They will "outmaneuver you and outsmart you!" One breeder says, "They want to please, but they want to please you *their* way."

Dals are very active dogs. They require a place to exercise. Although they are usually house dogs and do not do well left outside in extreme climates of hot or cold, they do need ample room to exercise on a daily basis to keep their high energy level under control. Either daily exercise or a fenced yard is a must. Dalmatians will follow a horse, a jogger, or a bicycle for miles. If left outside without companionship, he will become wild and unruly.

Dalmatians love activities which involve running, leaping and games. They chase squirrels and birds, balls and frisbees with equal enthusiasm. They will chase children if they are running. Young children are often overpowered by a Dalmatian which may leap above their heads and bound around them with seemingly endless energy. Dals can be fun for older children who are large enough to interact with an outgoing dog and enjoy a good romp. But remember, establish rules early about what you will allow the dog to do. A chasing puppy may be fun, but will you enjoy being chased by a full grown Dalmatian of sixty pounds? If not, don't let the puppy do it. We will talk more about this in the chapter on training, but the rule of thumb is "If you don't want the adult dog to do it, don't let him do it as a puppy."

A Dalmatian seems to have springs on his back legs. This leaping sometimes results in fence-jumping. A four foot high fence may not be adequate. Most of our breeders suggest five or six foot fences. Agility and intelligence may lead to fence climbing, especially with chain link fences. One breeder solved it by putting vinyl slats in the chain link to prevent the Dal from getting toe holds in the fence. Another breeder recommends a common stock electric wire around the top to keep the dog from jumping and hanging on the top edge of the fence. Many breeders suggest six foot wooden fencing for both privacy and insurance against climbers/leapers.

Especially during adolescence, Dals are great chewers and diggers. One breeder said she had raised a male "who started his own China trade route in the backyard." Some breeders have solved the problem by giving Dals areas where they are encouraged to dig, a sand pile or old barrel filled with dirt or sand. If they are encouraged to bury toys or bones in a specific area, they often leave the rest of the yard alone.

Barking is usually a problem resulting from inactivity or inattention. Dalmatians are social animals who love human companionship and will

Good fencing is a must to contain a Dalmatian.

bark if they are left alone for long periods of time. They can be vocal when interacting with the family. Many of them will "talk" using various throaty sounds. They will give alarm if something unusual is happening or if a stranger approaches. One breeder relates a story about a lovely dog, a finished champion who had done a number of personal appearances and had always been at ease with strangers in general. While on vacation, the van was threatened by two men who appeared to be trying to break in. When they later returned to the scene, the Dalmatian not only remembered them, but attacked with a deep throated "roar" such as he had never done before in his life.

A well-bred Dalmatian should not be hyperactive. Once mature and well socialized they often become couch potatoes and are very satisfied curling up on the couch next to their person. They should not be "bouncing off the walls," as one breeder puts it. And although they often pick a person in the family who is "special" to them, they are not specifically one-person dogs.

If you have other animals, Dalmatians are usually very good about accepting them as part of the family. Almost any animal, from cat to hamster, which is introduced to a Dal pup before he is three months old, will be accepted as part of the family.

Dals have very retentive memories. This is one reason they learn so fast. They will pick up tricks and obedience through repetition. Unfortunately, they will also learn things they should not. For example, a Dalmatian who does not live with children, but meets a child who teases him, will not forget the experience, especially if it happens on several occasions. The Dalmatian will generalize his negative attitude to other children. It is therefore important that these experiences are kept positive. Many of our breeders mentioned Dals and children particularly because the movie *One Hundred and One Dalmatians* and "Sparky" the fire dog have attracted kids of all ages to the breed.

Whatever you are doing, the Dalmatian is happy to be part of it. If a human is eating it, he wants some. If the game is Fetch, Frisbee or Hide and Seek, he wants to play. Even dress-up is fine as long as he can be part of the human group activity.

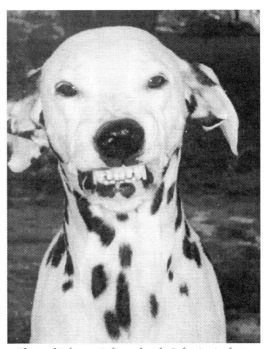

This "smile" does not indicate that the Dalmatian is about to attack.

Hugging and kissing are part of the breed. They will wrap their legs around their humans. They will also "smile." This ability, present in several, but certainly not all breeds, occurs when the dog is happy, ashamed, or trying to attract attention, depending on the dog. The lips are pulled up and back, showing the teeth. Sometimes the mouth is open slightly, and sometimes the eyes are narrowed. This is not the same as showing the teeth in defense, and is not a sign that the dog is about to bite. Not all Dalmatians will *smile*, but many do and it is sometimes difficult for those who have never seen the action in a dog to accept that it is not a threatening gesture.

All dogs within the breed are NOT alike. Not only are there

differences between individual dogs, even within the same litter, but within the breed there are differences in "styles." We will talk more about style within the course of this book. You will find some differences in Dalmatians in different regions of the country. Look through the Hall of Fame and see what dogs appeal to you, then look at the pedigrees. See if there are similar kennel names or dogs listed in the pedigrees. Talk to breeders about the things you like in the dogs you see and ask how their dogs compare. This is the beginning of being an educated buyer who will be happy with the dog he buys.

Do you prefer a male or female and why? Sex preference is usually a combination of personal taste and past experiences. Some breeders prefer males over females, especially for the show ring. Females tend to have "moods" which reflect their heat cycle and hormone fluctuations. Males are often considered more solid in temperament, with little day-to-day variation.

Spaying eliminates this mood swing problem, and most breeders, the SPCA, the AKC, and this editorial staff highly recommend spaying or neutering pets. Contrary to popular belief, spaying or neutering does not change a basic personality, nor does it make a dog fat and lazy. It does eliminate some of the swings in personality associated with hormones, such as males wandering off or becoming aggressive when they smell a female in heat, and female mood swings associated with the heat cycle. It also is much healthier for the dog or bitch, eliminating or reducing several types of cancer. Older bitches who get bred accidently may develop severe problems during pregnancy, including autoimmune syndrome. Spaying her early will prevent these health problems. Neutering is usually more expensive in a female than a male, but any animal not used for breeding should be neutered.

Two or more males may fight among themselves as they reach maturity and try to establish dominance. But two females may also fight, and one breeder suggests that females will "battle to the death" and have long memories about past enemies. Males will cool off when separated and will run and play together later. If you have a dog already, adding one of the opposite sex will probably work out best.

Males will lift their legs when mature. People sometimes feel this leads them to be harder to housebreak, which is not true. Males will often "mark" their territory. But females are often territorial, and it is not unknown to see a female who lifts her leg in this kind of behavior. Some breeders feel that a female wants to please more than their male counterparts. Males are sometimes seen as more frisky and outgoing, which is desirable for some owners. Males may be more lovable without being "pushy." They are not as demanding as females and although they like the attention, they will lie at your feet, or shadow you around the house. Females are sometimes a pest about attention, nagging and demanding attention when they want it, not necessarily when it is convenient for you to give it.

Consider that there may be a difference in price, depending on the demand and the breeder. Females are generally more expensive, and most likely to come with restrictions such as spaying contracts, limited registration (see the chapter on paperwork) or with a rider for breeding and puppies back. (See the chapter on finding a breeder.) If you're flexible about the sex, you may have an easier time, or find a good quality dog from a good breeder for a lower price.

SHOULD YOU BUY A DALMATIAN? ✧ 23

Dalmatians come in two coat colors: liver and black. Liver dogs are white with liver brown spotting, while blacks are white with black spots. Spots should be distinct, not intermingled, round and well defined in the size of a dime to a half-dollar. The spots should be evenly distributed without too many overlapping. Puppies with too little spotting or too heavy spotting, will be sold as pets and you might consider these dogs if you are not looking for a show dog.

Breeders disagree as to whether there is a difference in health and/or temperament between livers and blacks. One breeder suggests that livers are more "catlike" in personality, while blacks are more effusive. This aloof and dignified characteristic in livers is noted by other breeders also, who feel the blacks are more outgoing, tend to be clowns, and are more bubbly. Other breeders see no difference and point out that both colors come from the same lines and should be no different.

Many people, including some pet buyers, feel that black and white is somehow more of what a Dalmatian should look like. Livers seem to be a color that people either like or don't like. Some breeders felt it was harder to place livers, although other breeders felt they were more desirable because the color was not as common. If you have a strong preference for color, be sure to discuss it with your breeder. Most breeders did not feel color was a good basis for choosing a dog. They suggested that overall quality, temperament and health should be the primary basis for selecting a dog.

Finding and buying the right dog is an important first step. But remember, training, time, socialization and environment will be important factors in producing a well mannered dog who is a pleasure to live with and a fine family member for years to come.

THE STANDARD

*E*very breed which shows anywhere in the world has a written Standard of the Breed by which the dog is judged. This standard is important in preserving "breed type," or in layman's terms, those characteristics which make a Dalmatian a Dalmatian and not a Labrador Retriever!

The Standard is revised from time to time, and may vary from one country to another, but the main portion of the standard will be remarkably similar because they are describing the same breed. When a Standard is revised, only small, technical changes will be made. These changes will usually be important to show breeders, but not of particular importance to the general fancier of the breed, working kennels or pet owners. Even when the Standard is changed, a Dalmatian will still look like a Dalmatian.

The Standard for the Dalmatian was approved July 11, 1989, and effective September 6, 1989.

General Appearance - The Dalmatian is a distinctively spotted dog; poised and alert; strong, muscular and active; free of shyness; intelligent in expression; symmetrical in outline; and without exaggeration or coarseness. The Dalmatian is capable of great endurance, combined with a fair amount of speed.

Deviations from the described ideal should be penalized in direct proportion to the degree of deviation.

Size, Proportion, Substance - Desirable height at the withers is between 19 and 23 inches. Undersize or oversize is a fault. Any dog or bitch over 24 inches at the withers is disqualified.

The overall length of the body from the forechest to the buttocks is approximately equal to the height at the withers.

The Dalmatian has good substance and is strong and sturdy in bone, but never coarse.

Head - The head is in balance with the overall dog. It is of fair length and is free of loose skin. The Dalmatian's expression is alert and intelligent, indicating a stable and outgoing temperament.

The eyes are set moderately well apart, are medium sized and somewhat rounded in appearance, and are set well into the skull. Eye color is brown or blue, or any combination thereof; the darker the better and usually darker in black-spotted than in liver-spotted dogs.

Abnormal position of the eyelids or eyelashes (ectropion, entropion, trichiasis) is a major fault.

Incomplete pigmentation of the eye rims is a major fault.

The ears are of moderate size, proportionately wide at the base and gradually tapering to a rounded tip. They are set rather high, and are carried close to the head, and are thin and fine in texture. When the Dalmatian is alert, the top of the ear is level with the top of the skull and the tip of the ear reaches to the bottom line of the cheeks.

The top of the skull is flat with a slight vertical furrow and is approximately as wide as it is long. The stop is moderately well defined. The cheeks blend smoothly into a powerful muzzle, the top of which is level and parallel to the top of the skull. The muzzle and the top of the skull are about equal in length.

The nose is completely pigmented on the leather, black in black-spotted dogs and brown in liver-spotted dogs. Incomplete nose pigmentation is a major fault.

The lips are clean and close fitting. The teeth meet in a scissors bite. Overshot or undershot bites are disqualifications.

Neck, Topline, Body - The neck is nicely arched, fairly long, free from throatiness, and blends smoothly into the shoulders.

The topline is smooth.

The chest is deep, capacious and of moderate width, having good spring of rib without being barrel shaped. The brisket reaches to the elbow. The underline of the rib cage curves gradually into the moderate tuck-up.

The back is level and strong. The loin is short, muscular and slightly arched. The flanks narrow through the loin. The croup is nearly level with the back.

The tail is a natural extension of the topline. It is not inserted too low down. It is strong at the insertion and tapers to the tip, which reaches to the hock. It is never docked. The tail is carried with a slight upward curve but should never curl over the back. Ring tails and low-set tails are faults.

Forequarters - The shoulders are smoothly muscled and well laid back. The upper arm is approximately equal in length to the shoulder blade and joins it at an angle sufficient to insure that the foot falls under the shoulder. The elbows are close to the body. The legs are straight, strong and sturdy in bone. There is a slight angle at the pastern denoting flexibility.

Hindquarters - The hindquarters are powerful, having smooth, yet well defined muscles. The stifle is well bent. The hocks are well let down. When the Dalmatian is standing, the hind legs, when viewed from the rear are parallel to each other from the point of the hock to the heel of the pad. Cowhocks are a major fault.

Feet - Feet are very important. Both front and rear feet are round and compact with thick, elastic pads and well arched toes. Flat feet are a major fault. Toenails are black and/or white in black-spotted dogs and brown and/or white in liver-spotted dogs. Dewclaws may be removed.

Coat - The coat is short, dense, fine and close-fitting. It is neither wooly nor silky. It is sleek, glossy and healthy in appearance.

Color and Markings - Color and markings and their overall appearance are very important points to be evaluated.

The ground color is pure white. In black-spotted dogs the spots are dense black. In liver-spotted dogs the spots are liver brown. Any color markings other than black or liver are disqualified.

Spots are round and well defined, the more distinct the better. They vary from the size of a dime to the size of a half-dollar. They are pleasingly and evenly distributed. The less the spots intermingle the better. Spots are usually smaller on the head, legs and tail than on the body. Ears are preferably spotted.

Tri-color (which occurs rarely in this breed) is a disqualification. It consists of tan markings found on the head, neck, chest, leg or tail of a black-spotted or liver-spotted dog. Bronzing of black spots and fading and/or darkening of liver spots due to environmental conditions or normal processes of coat change are not tri-coloration.

Patches are a disqualification. A patch is a solid mass of black or liver hair containing no white hair. It is appreciably larger than a normal sized spot. Patches are a dense, brilliant color with sharply defined smooth edges. Patches are present at birth. Large color masses formed by intermingled or overlapping spots are not patches. Such masses should indicate individual spots by uneven edges and/or white hairs scattered throughout the mass.

Gait - In keeping with the Dalmatian's historical use as a coach dog, gait and endurance are of great importance. Movement is steady and effortless. Balanced angulation fore and aft combined with powerful muscles and good condition produce smooth efficient action. There is a powerful drive from the rear, coordinated with extended reach in the front. The topline remains level. Elbows, hocks and feet turn neither in nor out. As the speed of the trot increases, there is a tendency to single track.

Temperament - The temperament is stable and outgoing, yet dignified. Shyness is a major fault.

SCALE OF POINTS

General Appearance	5
Size, Proportion, Substance	10
Head	10
Neck, Topline, Body	10
Forequarters	5
Hindquarters	5
Feet	5
Coat	5
Color and Markings	25
Gait	10
Temperament	10
Total	**100**

Disqualifications

Any dog or bitch over 24 inches at the withers.
Overshot or undershot bite.
Any color markings other than black or liver.
Tri-color.
Patches.

All of this is a very complicated way to tell a breeder, judge or enthusiast what a Dalmatian looks like. Some of these terms are historical to the breed, such as "spots should not intermingle" or "neither wooly nor silky" having been used to describe the breed from the earliest times. Other terms, such as "good spring of rib" and "topline is smooth," and "hocks well let down" are dog show terms found in the standards of many breeds and meaning particular things to those who are used to reading standards and judging and evaluating dogs. Finally, some of the terms refer to anatomical parts of the dog, such as "pastern" and "stop" and "loin." For a breeder of quality dogs, it is his blueprint for breeding future generations to ensure that each generation will indeed be clearly recognizable as a Dalmatian. If you are going to take the time to educate yourself about a breed, the energy to find a breeder, and the money to purchase a purebred dog, it should have the characteristics of that breed and be a good representative of it. If it does not, any crossbred would have done just as well. There is no point to owning a purebred of such poor quality that it does not carry the characteristics typical of its breed.

"Style" is a term used to describe the variations between dogs, all of whom meet the standard. The standard is open to interpretation because it includes such words as "gradually," "slight" and "fair length." These words leave some room for a difference of opinion. How much is slight? How wide is sufficient? Combine these words with the fact that the standard describes the ideal dog and individual dogs will conform and deviate from the ideal to different degrees and in different manners. There is some room for judgment and personal preference.

If a dog has a lovely head and neck, for example, but does not move as well as another dog with wonderful movement but a head and neck that are not quite as lovely, different judges will penalize these faults differently depending on their preference. A judge who feels sound, good movement is the most important quality because the Dalmatian was bred to be an endurance dog will place the latter dog higher while a judge who feels that good heads and necks define the breed and that good moving dogs can be found in any breed, will place the former dog higher. A judge who feels that "...great endurance, combined with a fair amount of speed" is of utmost importance is likely to favor a lighter dog with more graceful lines over a heavy dog he might consider "coarse." But a different judge might read "...strong, muscular..." and consider the lighter dog to be "lacking substance." Although every good breeder and judge will read and understand the entire standard, they will have slightly different opinions of the words, phrases and emphasis of the standard. This is what gives rise to the different "styles" within the breed.

Countries, geographic areas of the United States, and different kennels and bloodlines will have a different look. You can see some of these differences by comparing the pictures in the Hall of Fame. Heads are easy to see in the photos and a careful study will reveal differences in the muzzle, for example. You may not be able to identify *why* some dogs are more appealing to you than others, but by looking at the pedigrees you should be able to see some similarities between the dogs you like and their common ancestors.

Because each breeder puts an emphasis on different words within the Standard and interprets the Standard differently, and because no dog is perfect, breeders will select their breeding stock based on what they feel the standard means when it describes the perfect dog. The breeder selects generation after generation based on qualities he feels are the most important and gradually his dogs begin to look alike, though not *exactly* like those of another kennel. Sometimes breeders become very opinionated about why their version of the breed is "right" and why other breeders' dogs are "wrong." All of this is a way of saying that although a Dalmatian should look like a Dalmatian, not all Dalmatians will look **exactly** alike.

No dog is perfect, but a good breeder strives to improve the quality of his dogs with each generation. When a breeder makes a breeding, he will consider the pedigree and the individual dog. He will attempt to breed dogs which are strong in one area to dogs who are strong in other areas in the attempt to get a dog which is strong in both areas. Breeding a dog with a timid temperament or poor topline to one with similar faults, which often happens in backyard breeding (because the breeder does not know the difference), will only result in an entire litter with the same faults!

The Dalmatian, as described in the standard, is a medium size dog, solid looking, never frail or slight. The first impression when looking at a Dalmatian is of a strong, well-muscled, alert animal with unique markings. It should give an impression of sturdiness, durability and endurance. The Dalmatian should **not** look coarse, overdone, too large, nor should it look delicate or fragile.

The striking thing is the color, which should be white with well defined spots of liver or black. The overall outline is a little like a hound, having long ears, a medium long neck, and a head with some drop from the top of the head to the muzzle (stop). The nose should not be pointed (snippy). The back is straight, not lumpy, if seen in profile. The tail is long, and just about the right length to knock things off the coffee table. It wags frequently, and can be whiplike when it knocks against the leg of a human. Correct movement is very important for this breed since endurance and a ground covering stride were historic requirements.

The height is nineteen to twenty-three inches, with dogs over twenty-four inches to be disqualified. Most males will rub the upper limit of size while most bitches are an inch or two shorter. This means the Dalmatian will be knee high or slightly taller on the average person. Although there is no indication of weight, a Dalmatian is described as being solid looking. This means that fifty-five to sixty-five pounds for males, forty-five to fifty-five pounds for females will be approximately the correct weight. If the dog is too much heavier it will look fat or clumsy (coarse) and too much lighter it will look frail or spindly (lacks substance). All of our breeders agree that the most common cause for a dog being disqualified from the show ring (meaning it cannot be shown again if the dog is disqualified for the same problem under three different judges) is being oversized — over twenty-four inches at the withers. This is also one of the most common reasons for a dog to be a pet. Breeders will place puppies which look like they will be too large, and sometimes this is even a reason a nice adult dog is for sale instead of continuing his show career. Many breeders have had the experience of having a nice pup grow too large. Sometimes the Dal has begun to show as a pup, perhaps even winning points, until he grows too large to remain under the size limit called for in the standard.

Large spots, smudged spots, fuzzy spots (ticking) or spots which are smaller than a dime or larger than a half-dollar are not desirable. Smudged white, or buff tone on the white is not desirable. Both liver and black are equally acceptable, and personal preference is the only basis for favoring one color over the other. Eyes are black, dark brown or blue with black eye rims in black and white dogs; golden brown, hazel, light brown or blue with brown eye rims in the liver dogs. The nose should be black in the black dogs; brown in the liver dogs. Patches are spots larger than a half-dollar, with no white hairs. Sometimes it is difficult to tell the difference between a patch, which is a disqualification, and a "group of spots." Think of throwing a group of coins onto a table. They will group up and overlap, but you will still see the outlines and indication of the individual circles. This grouping is acceptable, but a solid spot like a pool of syrup spilled

This dog has nice structure — that is he is well put together — but his spotting is much too heavy for show.

onto the table is not. The syrup may be irregular in shape, but it is solid, not made up of a series of individual small circles. A patch is a puddle of dense, brilliant color with sharply defined, smooth edges. Patches on the ears and around the eyes are reported to be the most common. Tri-color, as was found in some of the early dogs, is not acceptable. A Tri-color dog has light tan or lemon spots on the head, neck, chest, leg or tail, and black or liver spots on the rest of the body. Dogs with lemon or light tan spots are **not** acceptable.

Blue eyes are not unusual in Dalmatians. They are not a disqualifying fault, and a dog may have one or two blue eyes. It is a matter of personal preference if you like the look of blue eyes instead of traditional dark eyes. Blue eyes are **not** blind, and although there are some rumors, at this time there is no proven correlation between blue eyes and deafness.

The tail should not be tucked under the stomach which indicates a shy temperament. It should be carried up and out in a fine, outgoing attitude. It should be straight, not curled, and have short hair, not long fringe along the underside.

The breed has stayed essentially the same over the years. Modern breeders like a square dog, though traditionally the Dalmatian was slightly longer than tall. Often a dog moves better when the back is a little longer because the rear legs can drive up under the dog without overtaking the front feet. With a short back, if the rear legs reach too far up under the body, they may interfere with the movement of the front legs, and often a dog will twist the front legs (paddling, winging) or roll the shoulders in order to get the front feet out of the way of the rear ones. Temperaments have improved over the last twenty years according to breeders and judges alike. Pigmentation has become darker and more solid around the eyes and nose.

Dogs from one area of the country will vary from those in other areas of the country. Our breeders say that those in the East and South are lighter and have somewhat more leg than those in the West. One problem with showing in a different area of the country is that if all the dogs in the ring are elegant and good movers, a heavier dog will appear coarse by comparison. However, if all the dogs are large, a lighter dog will appear to have a lack of substance and look out of place by comparison.

Sometimes a dog will be a top winner, making him a popular choice for stud service. In time, there will be a lot of pups with a similar look showing. This is one way that style changes happen. Try to choose a breeder who remains true to his mental picture of what the Dalmatian should look like and does not change direction with every new winner.

"Strong" is a key word in the standard for a pet owner. That strength, combined with the size of the dog, is one reason why early obedience training is a must. A sixty pound, strong puppy can easily drag an owner down the street if he does not have the training and the manners to walk without pulling, leaping or running out to the end of the leash every time something catches his eye. The wild ride in the opening scene of *One Hundred and One Dalmatians* may have been funny to view on the screen, but it is not something most owners want to experience! You should enjoy walking your dog, not have him enjoy walking you and early obedience training is important in order to insure a well-mannered adult.

This liver color is acceptable according to the standard.

FINDING A BREEDER

Once you have determined what you intend to do with the dog, and think that the Dalmatian may be right for your home, contact several breeders. They will be able to give you a detailed idea of how they see the breed. Ask them about situations specific to your lifestyle and living conditions and see if they feel the breed — and their dogs — will do well in those circumstances. These questions about specific situations will help you determine if the breed is right for you, instead of asking general questions about the breed and hearing a breeder's glowing report about why he thinks Dalmatians are wonderful dogs. Assume — by virtue of the fact that he is breeding Dalmatians and not Rottweilers — the breeder is dedicated to and loves the Dalmatian. But you need to establish some way to measure if the breed will be RIGHT FOR YOU. No single breed is perfect for everyone. People breed and buy purebred dogs so that there is some predictability of what the puppy will be like. Use that predictability to determine if you will be happy with the pup or older dog BEFORE you buy. You will be happier, the match between owner and dog will be better, and it will make for a happier life for everyone concerned. A good match between family and dog also helps to eliminate a good dog ending up in an animal shelter. One of our breeders said, "I am annoyed when people spend more time looking into the qualities of a TV set or computer than they do into a dog. The dog will come into their homes and be part of their lives for more years than either appliance will last!"

Ask your breeder about the standard, how his dogs match and where the particular puppy may deviate. A standard is very important to breeders because it gives them something written against which to measure their dog. Without a written standard, a breed would change freely at the whim of what was popular with judges and fanciers at the time. The standard pulls the breed back to the middle of the range, but individual dogs will vary in some ways. In fact, there is seldom a dog who matches the standard perfectly. Breeding with the standard in mind is one thing that marks the difference between "Good Breeders" and "Puppy Mills," or uneducated "Backyard Breeders." Breeders who take the time and trouble to learn their breed, to evaluate their dogs, and to make breedings which will keep their puppies in the range where they are still easily recognizable as their breed are those who best ensure the future of the Dalmatian. These breeders are best able to predict if a puppy will grow up to be representative of his breed in conformation and temperament, and if you will be pleased to spend years of your life with him.

Often pet owners will ask why it should make any difference to them if a breeder breeds to the standard. The reason is quite obvious. If, as a new owner, you have taken the time to look into the breed, you have a right to a dog which will grow up to be recognizable as that breed. As long as a dog has AKC papers, and it is bred to a bitch with AKC papers and the paperwork is in order, AKC will issue papers for the puppies. But that does not ensure that those puppies will indeed grow up to be representative of their breed. For that, you must trust your breeder. Generations of breeding without regard to the standard will produce puppies which, at best, are barely recognizable as the breed. If you already own a Dalmatian, look at the photos in the Hall of Fame section and see how your dog compares. Are there similar names to those in your dog's pedigree or at lease similar kennel names? When buying a dog, look at the parents, if possible, and see if you like them and if you feel they represent what you are looking for in the breed. If you are buying long distance, look at photos of the sire and dam. Compare these dogs to the outstanding examples of the breed we have featured in the Hall of Fame.

Many Dalmatian breeders refer to the Disney features *One Hundred and One Dalmatians* simply as "The Movies." These movies have increased the demand for Dalmatians with each release. This has led to a proliferation of backyard breeders and puppy mill operations. Though this is never good for any breed, it is especially bad for Dalmatians and has led to a proliferation of bad temperaments and health problems.

Many pet shops have Dalmatians. Purchasing a puppy from a pet shop is often an impulse buy. While shopping, people see a cute puppy and suddenly decide to buy it without looking into the breed or taking a careful look at their home situation which can lead to disaster. Most pet shops buy their pups from "Puppy Mills," which breed any dog with papers to any bitch with papers without regard to the quality of the dog or how representative it may be for its breed. They seldom have the kind of early puppy socialization and handling that those from a breeder will have experienced. A puppy learns important "social skills" from the mother and the littermates, as well as from the early human contact. This socialization is something that a puppy mill puppy does not get since he is raised in a cage, usually without human contact, and removed early from his litter to be sent as soon as possible to the distributor or wholesaler and on to the pet shop while he is still young enough to be "cute." From a more practical standpoint, puppy mill puppies are often raised in close confinement where they learn to soil close to where they eat. Once this pattern overrides the dog's natural desire to be clean and keep his "living area" free of waste, he will be much harder to housetrain!

Pet shop prices will be as high or higher than those of a reputable breeder, but the quality will certainly be lower. It is not likely that you will find a well-bred pup of good temperament in a pet store, since breeders, by their code of ethics, do not sell to pet stores. A good breeder will want to personally meet, to screen and to match each pup with each home. This leads to a better fit between family and dog and a happier life for everyone. Sometimes people are surprised that a reputable breeder will also not donate a puppy as a raffle or door prize, even for a good cause. The reason is because it is important to a good breeder that the puppy fit the home, and he wants to reserve the right to make that decision *before* the puppy leaves. Reputable breeders sell their puppies to good homes and they do not produce more puppies than they are able to sell. An experienced breeder is the best source for a well-bred puppy which has been well-socialized.

For these humanitarian reasons, and because of many new laws which widen the scope of responsibility for the retailer, many pet shops, including some of the large chains, no longer carry puppies.

Another avenue is to buy a puppy advertised in the newspaper. Here, at least, the buyer has had time to think about whether he really wants a puppy instead of making an impulse buy. He had to get out the paper, look for an ad, call for information and make a special trip to the breeder's home. These puppies will be cheaper than those from a good breeder or a pet shop because these private individuals have no other outlet for placing their puppies. Reputable breeders sometimes sell their pups through the newspaper, but the vast majority of newspaper ads will be from backyard breeders. These people have often simply bred their bitch to any local stud. Just because someone has puppies for sale doesn't make him a breeder. He may have no idea of the breeding behind the dogs, what kinds of health problems may be lurking in the pedigree ready to affect the puppies, or how to match traits of the parents in order to ensure that the puppies are of good quality. These puppies are cheap, but they usually do not carry any health guarantee. Even in states which require the breeder to be responsible for the puppy's health, these backyard breeders are exempted because they do not produce more than one or two litters a year. You can end up spending more money on vet bills than you save and may still not end up with a good specimen.

Many breed clubs advise people that the WORST first step is to go and look at a litter of puppies from the local newspaper. Chances are you will fall in love with the adorable pups and your heart may overrule your head.

In short, a pet shop will be expensive for the quality you receive, but there will be a health guarantee of some kind. A backyard breeder will usually not have any kind of guarantee, and the pups may be of mixed quality in terms of health and conformation. These are the types of purchases which most frequently end up with a mismatched dog and home and where the owner later decides to drop the dog off at the SPCA or give him away. Take your time and look for a reputable breeder. You will pay about what you would pay for the pet shop puppy, and you will get not only a guarantee, but a good representation of a Dalmatian, and you will have some idea about the style and temperament of the puppy before you buy.

TAKE YOUR TIME AND DO YOUR HOMEWORK. This will ensure that you end up with a dog which will be a good companion for many years to come. It is important to buy from a reputable breeder in all breeds, but the Dalmatian is one of the breeds where it is particularly important. Deafness or poor temperament often plague poorly bred pups. Temperament has improved greatly within the last twenty years with good breeders, but many dogs of poor quality still exhibit the traits which at one time gave the Dalmatian a bad name as a family pet. Although a well-bred Dalmatian is intelligent and solid in temperament, the poorly bred dog may be nervous, barking continuously and hyperactive to the point that his attention span is too short for him to be able to learn even the most basic lessons in good behavior. A careful, knowledgeable breeder pays attention to temperament when making his breedings. He can provide you with a puppy which has all the traits and temperament qualities which brought this breed to the forefront of popularity around the world!

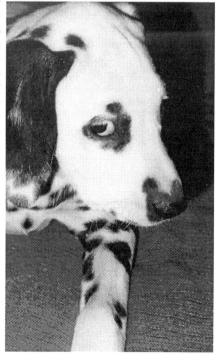

A quality breeder may breed only one or two litters a year, or he may have puppies fairly frequently. The number of puppies produced is not the issue; it is the care which is put into the breeding and into developing a breeding program. It is how knowledgeable he is about their bloodlines and how willing he is to provide you with both good and bad information about the breed and the lines which makes the difference. It is the help he can give you in selecting a puppy which will fit into your home and the support a good breeder will give you throughout the lifetime of the dog which is important. And it is the care he has taken to produce a dog of great beauty, sound temperament and good health which make these puppies well worth the additional money. Good breeders always strive to make the next generation better than the last.

Several of our breeders are concerned about newspaper ads which advertise "white Dalmatians" or "rare lemon/rare yellow Dalmatians." All Dalmatian puppies are born white and get their spots as they get older. In well marked dogs, these spots show up well before the puppy is eight weeks old and ready for sale. Lemon or yellow, any spotting of a paler color than a dark, rich liver brown is a major fault. Sometimes out of ignorance, sometimes out of greed, unscrupulous breeders will try to get more money, or sell pups of this inferior quality by claiming they are "rare." Or they may simply have light colored pups whose spots do not show up well until they are several months old because of their pale color. The owner may be too ignorant to know that the pups will get color later. Stay away from these pups. If the breeder does not know enough about the breed to know this is an undesirable color, how will he know enough to produce a good quality puppy of sound temperament and good health? Buying such a puppy is an invitation to disaster. The most striking quality of the Dalmatian is the unusual color. It should be a striking contrast between white and the densely colored spots. Why settle for anything less?

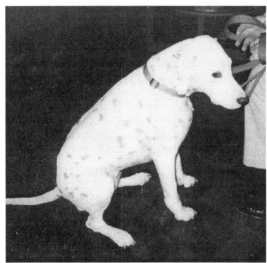

This lemon Dalmatian is an uncommon color only because it is not a recognized color for the breed. Never pay more for a lemon pup because you are told it is a "rare" color.

All puppies are wonderful. They have the same cuteness about them that babies have, but as with babies, not everyone is ready to take on the responsibility of raising a puppy. Like babies, puppies take time and special attention. They will make mistakes, not just in house training, but in deciding what is proper to chew, when to come and when to follow their own curiosity. They may be exuberant about life and playful when you are tired and want to settle into a chair and relax. Dalmatians take two to three years to mature, settle down and relax. Be sure you can live through the growing period before you take on raising a Dalmatian.

Dalmatians are busy and curious. They will open doors and look in, and if left undisciplined, they may inspect the top of the kitchen table to see what has been left there. They may be avid gardeners, rearranging the flower beds enthusiastically. Prepare yourself to do early training with the puppy or new dog so that you can get off to a good, sound start in the relationship.

Dalmatians adapt to a variety of homes as long as they have human companionship. They do need exercise on a regular basis. If they do not have space to run and play in a yard, they must be taken for frequent walks, and preferably have a park or area where they can run loose and play with other dogs. They love to be petted and played with, using almost any sort of play activity or toy.

If you have time, go to a local dog show and see all the different breeds in the ring. Go early and plan to stay all day, wandering from ring to ring and looking at the breeds you are interested in seeing. Or go sometime in the early afternoon to see the Groups which are held at the end of the judging day, usually starting around two o'clock, depending on the size of the show. Here, the single best representative of each breed will compete in one of seven different groups. The group winners will return at the end of the day for the judging of Best in Show.

Don't expect to see puppies at a dog show. Good breeders — and AKC rules — keep puppies at home where they belong. Breeders are there for the sport, not for the purpose of selling puppies, so the attitude of breeders selling you a puppy will not be the same as those of a pet shop. In a pet shop, you are the customer and it is their business to sell you a puppy. With a breeder, this is his sport or hobby. He has no trouble selling the puppies he offers for sale each year, and he is more concerned with matching the puppy with the new home to ensure a long and happy relationship for both the new owner and the dog, than in getting your money. Because of that, he is less likely to act as if you are the valued customer. Remember that when you deal with a breeder. Breeders look at their pups as part of their family, and part of your family. Their role is closer to that of a social worker handling an adoption than a retail business which is selling a product to a customer. There are no two dogs alike, and they are not something which can be ordered or fixed like an inanimate object offered in a store or catalog.

It is sometimes difficult to talk to breeders at a show because they may be busy getting their dogs ready for the ring. Most show people take these shows very seriously and therefore they may be short of small talk at the show. Remember that these exhibitors have a lot invested in the show at hand in terms of entry fees, travel and perhaps handling expenses and advertising. Selling you a puppy or helping you find one is not likely to be their first priority the day of the show.

However, a dog show is a good place to find names and addresses of breeders. A catalog of the show will list the name of the entry, the owner or owners and an address, the name of the breeder, the sire and dam of the entry, the whelping date of the entry and sometimes the name of the "agent," or person actually showing the entry on that day. By watching the classes, you can see what to expect of a Dalmatian at different ages, how they develop, and by looking at sires and dams, and then looking at the dogs in the ring, you will begin to see family resemblances in different bloodlines, much as you

Dal pups are busy and curious, into almost everything.

can see them by looking at the pictures in the Hall of Fame. The address of the owner may be listed under the name of the dog, or it may be in the back of the book where all owners for all breeds are listed alphabetically. When you get home, call directory information for the phone number or write for information and a contact phone number.

Local kennel clubs may have a listing of breeders in your area. Calling breeders listed in major dog publications is another way of beginning the process of finding a dog. We have featured breeders in the Hall of Fame who are knowledgeable in the breed and who will be willing to talk to you.

A good breeder, one who knows the bloodline and has watched the puppies from birth, will have be able to develop an idea of what will fit your lifestyle. Describe HOW you want the dog to fit into your household, what you expect it to do, and what your family is like. Ask the breeder how he or she feels on issues of importance to you. Listen carefully to the answers. Ask the breeder to list the most important factors in his breeding program. If health (or soundness) and temperament are not on the list — be careful. Then listen for those qualities you think will be important to you, such as intelligence, show quality, size and potential for training.

Each breeder will have his own ideas about what is the most important thing in a Dalmatian, or in other words, the "essence" of the breed. One breeder will focus on good coats, while another will focus on good heads. Each will select their breeding stock based on the area of importance to them. When a breeder adds new stock to his program, makes an "outside" breeding (one to a stud or bitch which is not owned by the kennel), or selects puppies to keep for the breeding and show program, the breeder will select animals which are strong in those areas which are of importance to him. That is why you will see a difference between the dogs or the "style" of different kennels.

Read through the Hall of Fame information. See if what the breeder says about his breeding program matches what you are looking for in a dog. When you talk to him on the phone, ask about his philosophy of breeding. Many breeders will simply say, "We breed for . . ." See if he is breeding for what you need in a dog.

In the end, you are often better off trusting the breeder to select a puppy for your family than in picking it yourself. You will see the puppies for only a short time. One may be tired after a morning of playing, it may have just eaten and be sleepy, or it may be awakened or be reacting to a littermate in an uncharacteristic manner. Puppies are like all siblings; they do not always bring out the best in one another, though generally they will get along.

The breeder has seen this litter for weeks, watching it and comparing it to other litters from the same bloodlines. He knows more about each puppy than you can possibly see within the framework of a short visit. Remember, the selection you make will be with you for many years so use sound judgment and as much information as you can find out before making the selection. This is like going to a stock broker, lawyer or insurance agent for advice rather than trying to handle such matters yourself by a quick, often unknowing, evaluation.

WHAT YOU SHOULD ASK A BREEDER

Be sure to ask how and where the pups have been raised. If you go to the kennel, is it clean and neat enough so the dogs are not living in life threatening situations? If you have pictures, look at the surroundings as well as at the puppy. Is it clean? Do the pups have a dry place to live and enough room so they can set up housekeeping without learning to be dirty? Can the breeder tell you why he thought his bitch was worth breeding and why he bred the litter? If it is the first litter, who was the breeder who helped him select his breeding stock and raise his litter? If there is not an experienced breeder helping, don't buy a pup, as the breeder does not

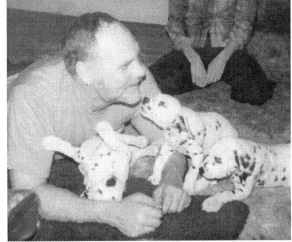

Socialization is an important part of raising a litter of well-adjusted puppies.

have enough knowledge to ensure that you will get a good puppy. If there is a "mentor" breeder, ask for a reference name and telephone number.

Never buy from someone who did not whelp and raise the litter. These kinds of people are "puppy brokers" and there is no telling what you may get.

Will the breeder be willing to help you if you have problems? How did he socialize the litter and at what age were the pups weaned? What kind of guarantee goes with the pup? If it is a female, are there "breeder's terms" which may require you to breed a litter? Will there be a written contract?

Do the dogs look healthy, well fed and in good spirits? Are they outgoing and do they seem to have an honest affection for the breeder? If you get down and try to play with them, will they react to you or avoid you? What kind of instructions, puppy starter kits, and paperwork will you receive when you take home a pup? At what age will a puppy go home?

Be sure to identify the qualities you want in a dog. Because temperament varies within the breed, between kennels, and between individuals, ask about how the breeder views the temperament of the breed in general, and this litter in particular. See how well the answers match your family's needs.

Don't seek conflicting qualities. An active, playful, outgoing dog is apt to be harder to train and harder on the house than one with a laid back personality which is basically quiet by nature. Dalmatians, in general, are active and merry. They will need firm, kind discipline from the beginning. If you have a house full of antiques, it is best not to look for the puppy who is the clown of the litter. He will be the one who will likely steal socks, carry off the toilet paper (which is still attached to the roll in the bathroom), rearrange the dried flower arrangement, and reconstruct the antique chair legs. Select the more sedate littermate who is more interested in being a quiet human companion. If you have young children, don't select the feisty one. If he stands up for his rights with his littermates, he may also stand up for his rights to the food bowl and toys if the baby approaches.

Ask the breeder what health problems may be present in the breed. If the breeder continuously states that there are no problems in health or temperament, no problems in training, and generally represents the dog to be nothing but a 100% ideal pet, beautiful enough to be a show dog but "I just want to find him a good home," be careful. While all responsible breeders are interested in finding their puppies a good home, they should also be able to evaluate their dogs and alert you to what you need to be aware of in dog ownership and ownership of a Dalmatian in particular. Individual dogs need training and socialization. Bloodlines have good points and bad points, and a good breeder will know both the strengths and weaknesses. "Kennel blind" breeders may run the risk of overlooking faults and thereby breeding them into the line. A breeder cannot strive to eliminate a problem if he is too kennel blind to see it.

If you are looking for a pet, be sure to ask WHY the puppy is selling as a pet. Be careful of breeders who give involved stories about why this is a perfect dog, but is being sold at a bargain price. As in any other field, these people know their product. Most reasons for a dog to be classified as a pet are of no concern to the average pet owner. A good breeder is producing dogs of such high quality that the small, critical points which will cause him to sell the dog as a pet will hardly be recognized at all by the average owner. The poorest quality dog from a good breeder will still be miles above those produced by a backyard breeder or a puppy mill.

Think of it in terms of basketball. If you are watching junior high school basketball, you may be able to pick out the best player. But that player will be infinitely inferior to an NBA player who has been dropped from the team for his lack of ability! Such is the difference between a puppy which is being cut by a breeder and sold as a pet (the professional player who has been dropped) and the best of what the backyard breeder or puppy mill will produce. Pets from a good breeder will run $400 to $500, with show dogs going higher, depending on their age and quality. You will pay the same from a pet shop. You may buy a pup from a backyard breeder for only $150 but consider that Dalmatians live for twelve to fifteen years and the annual allotments over that many years will make the savings minimal. One of our breeders reports a top producing male who was still active, producing puppies, and in perfect health at eleven and a half years. If you divide the extra cost by the number of years of the dog, you are paying only $16 to $20 more per year to have a really beautiful dog in good health and with a good temperament! It is like owning a Mercedes instead of a Geo Metro for only about $20 a year!

And, you may not even save that on a lower priced dog. Health problems, which the backyard breeder may be ignorant of, or the puppy mill breeder may not care about, may run the vet bills up much higher over the lifetime of the dog than the additional price of the dog.

When considering sex, realize that a bitch will have, as one breeder said, "raging hormones." This may cause her to have mood swings and to lose coat. If spayed, which most of our breeders highly recommend, this problem will be eliminated. If you are looking to keep down the cost of a dog, consider that neutering a male is cheaper than spaying a female.

Older dogs may be an alternative. Dalmatians adapt to almost any type of home, and an older, well mannered, well socialized dog may be an alternative if the family does not have a lot of time or patience for a puppy. If household members are not home during the day or if you are looking for a dog which is ready to play, travel, or show, you should look for an older dog. Pups need care, training, and rest and should not be taken out in public until after they have had a full set of shots. They may be too delicate or tire easily when playing with older children. If you are looking for a show dog, try to find an older dog which can be evaluated in terms of the finer points of conformation and movement. The older the dog is, and the more successful his parents and other litters of the same breeding have been, the higher the chances that he will be a show ring winner. Sometimes a breeder will keep two littermate brothers until they are old enough to see some fine points of adult conformation. Then the lesser brother will be sold to make room in the kennel. These dogs are a good buy because they are the very best of the litter.

Common show faults which will make a dog a pet are: off-bites (which may not show up until the permanent teeth are in), slip stifles (ask about this carefully and see the "health" chapter), low tail set, weak topline or high ear set (which will go almost undetected to anyone but a show breeder or judge), mismarking or undesirable show color, light brown eyes (as we have mentioned in the chapter on the standard), length of back, low in the leg, high in the rear, lack of substance or having restricted movement. Unless you have spent years with show dogs, these faults will be hard to see even if they are pointed out to you, though to the breeder they may be very obvious.

One of the most common reasons for a Dalmatian to be a pet is "patches." These large black (or sometimes white) spots mean that the pup does not have the correct color pattern to be a show dog. The oversize black spot is often on an ear, around an eye, or across the face. Although it will change the look of the pup, it sometimes adds character and many people do not mind the marking on a pet. Consider this as a possible type of pet. Another common show fault is going oversize. If the line is large, and this particular puppy is large for his age, a breeder may predict that the dog will go over the show limit. If you are used to big dogs, the additional size will probably not matter, but if you are looking for a small bitch on the short size of the standard, this will make a difference to you.

This dog is too dark to be a show dog but he will make a very nice pet.

One kind of pet you should **NOT** consider is a deaf dog. The **Dalmatian Club of America** has issued a call for all deaf dogs to be euthanised. Often people will feel like they can provide a "special home" for these handicapped dogs. When they are unable to take care of the dog, they feel guilty. According to DCA statistics, deafness occurs in 10%-12% of all Dalmatians, with this figure running lower with reputable breeders who are striving to eliminate the problem through testing of breeding stock and selective breeding, and higher for those who do not know or care about their breeding programs. It is estimated that half of all the registered dogs are produced by people who have never bred a litter before. For most of them, it will be their last attempt (See our last chapter on breeding.) It is difficult to expect these people to prevent, recognize and deal with the deafness problem since they have no experience to draw from.

The chapter on health will deal more with deafness, but we should say that it is not simply a matter of dogs who have no hearing. In a study by Dr. Alexander De Lahunta of Cornell University, and a doctoral thesis by Dr. Margaret Ferrara, an Australian breeder of Dalmatians, as stated in the January 1991 *Gazette* article by Elaine Waldorf Gewirts, "Researching Deafness in Dalmatians:" "*A deaf dog's brain is abnormal. Brain cells in both unilaterally and totally deaf Dals begin to deteriorate as early as the first day after being whelped. The neurons from the ear which becomes deaf are present, but degenerate before hearing is well established. (The puppy will be deaf by six weeks of age.) The degeneration of the neurons in the ear causes neurons in the brain to degenerate too.*"

Although the extent of this brain damage is difficult to determine, deaf dogs are not simply without hearing, they are often neurotic, nervous, paranoid and even aggressive. They are frequently out of control. One breeder who works with rescue

Dalmatians tells a story of one deaf dog which jumped up on the refrigerator and urinated! Well meaning people who try to provide homes for these dogs are usually faced with a situation which they cannot handle, even with patient care and a loving, supportive atmosphere. Good breeders never knowingly sell a deaf puppy, but it takes some experience to be able to determine. This will explain why the seemingly heartless policy of humanely putting down deaf pups is a difficult, but necessary approach to the problem.

Likewise, if you want a good looking, top quality dog, even if it is for a pet, do not expect a small price tag simply because you don't want to show. Often the same qualities which make an attractive dog a good show prospect also make it a particularly appealing pet. Remember, breeders price their puppies by quality or characteristics, not by purposes of the buyer. However, some breeders may insist that certain puppies be shown as part of the buying contract. Be sure to inquire about show contracts if you are seeking a top quality dog which is represented as being a show prospect. Also, sales of bitch puppies sometimes include a demand for puppies back to the breeder as part of the purchase price. Think about this carefully. It will obligate you to working with the breeder for many years to come, and commits you to breeding a litter of puppies in the future when you may not want to do so. You get all the work of raising a litter (see last chapter, "Breeding Your Dog,") and the breeder gets the best puppy or puppies!

If you are interested in showing or breeding the dog, you need to be honest about that up front. Don't try to get a show dog for a cheap price because you say it will be a pet. The worst possible thing to do is to tell a breeder you only want a pet, when in fact you have intentions of breeding it. First, consider carefully before you breed your dog. As we have outlined in the last chapter, it may not be the quick and easy money it looks like, nor the wonderful experience you envision. Second, there may be problems with the dog which the breeder did not reveal because it would not affect your puppy, but would make breeding inadvisable. Littermates may have carried defects or health problems. Although your dog may not be affected by the problem, and it was not mentioned since your dog was healthy, the breeder may sell the litter as pets because he realizes that there is a high chance the normal pups may carry the recessive gene and pass it along to their offspring. Then YOU are the breeder who has to deal with the problem which may be costly and result in loss of puppies or irate buyers who may purchase pups with problems that you do not have the experience to spot!

So, if you intend to breed, or even think you may breed, tell the breeder up front. Invest the money in a good dog or bitch. Be honest about what you want to do with the dog as this is the only way a breeder can do his job in helping you find the right dog for you and your family. Today AKC will allow breeders to mark papers as "non-breeding," which means that even though the dog or bitch you have purchased may carry AKC papers, puppies from that animal may not be registered, even if bred to another AKC registered animal. You, as the new owner, cannot change the registration after the purchase. This has been done to try to eliminate backyard breeding, and every year more breeders use this option for their pet puppies. (See chapter on paperwork for more information on this limited registration.)

Ask the breeder about spaying and neutering contracts. Ask what guarantee the breeder offers with the puppy. CAUTION: If you are seeking a show dog, don't expect a breeder to be able to pick out a group placing dog at eight weeks of age. These are few and far between, and a show dog is a product not only of his gene pool, but of environmental factors in his upbringing, how he is shown and conditioned, how he is presented in the ring, where he is shown, and what other dogs he is showing against on any given day.

Remember, if you are looking for an obedience or show ring winner, find a pedigree where the parents, other litters, and other dogs in the litter have excelled in those areas. A good pedigree is your best assurance that the puppy is likely to be successful in competition. Better yet, find an older puppy or young adult that can be evaluated in the ring or in the field.

Look at other adults in the kennel if you visit. See if they appear to be the kind of dog you are looking for. See the dam, and if possible, see the sire of the litter. These are usually a good indication of quality and characteristics of the puppy. One word of caution: After a bitch whelps, she may lose her hair. This is called "blowing coat." Some bitches do it worse than others so that you may hardly notice it on one bitch, yet another may look ratty and have bald spots. This is NOT an indication of skin problems. It does not mean that the pups will have skin problems. It is a phsysiological condition which is sometimes apparent in bitches after whelping, brought on by hormones released during whelping and lactation. Many breeders believe that it is caused by the protein which would normally go to hair growth being redirected to the milk for the puppies. If you see a bitch whose coat is in "ratty" condition, ask your breeder about it, but realize that it may be normal for this bitch.

The Dalmatian Club of Greater St. Louis Drill Team is made up of well-trained and well-adjusted Dalmatians.

BUYING A DOG LONG DISTANCE

Sometimes it is necessary to buy a dog a long distance. Don't panic. When you talk to a breeder on the phone, use the same technique you would use in person. Ask questions that will give you an idea of the experience of your breeder; how he feels about issues in the breed that are important to you and your family; how well he listens to why you want the dog; and how well he tries to match you with what he has available. Find one who enjoys his dogs, who knows what his bloodlines will produce, and who sounds like someone you can trust and have confidence in. Ask about guarantees and expectations. This is the same thing you should be doing with a local breeder, or one whose kennel you visit to see a litter. Also, see the chapter on shipping and travel.

WHAT NOT TO ASK A BREEDER

Don't ask a breeder what he thinks of another breeder by name. Ask for a reference if he has nothing available, but when you ask about another breeder by name, you may get more information about the politics within the breed and personal prejudices, both for and against, than real information about the quality of dogs being bred. One breeder may like a small dog and have nothing good to say about another breeder's larger dogs, without really giving the reason why there is a negative comment. Remember that dog breeding, showing and field trial competitions are just that — competitions. Over the years, disputes arise over wins and losses, or over personal issues that may have nothing to do with the quality of the dog or the purpose you have in mind for your pet. These "feuds" are carried over into what one breeder — and later his close friends — say about another breeder.

Don't begin your conversation by asking "How much?" It will depend on the puppy. Most breeders feel that the suitability of the dog to the home is the primary concern. If price is the bottom line for you, more important than inquiring about the dog or the breeder, you should probably not be getting a dog at all.

Do not expect to be able to go to a breeder's home for a Sunday visit if you are simply looking at the breed for future reference. While some breeders have this kind of time, most good breeders do not have hours to spend on people who visit as something to do for the day. If you are simply looking at the breed, you can do that at a dog show where you can see many examples of the breed.

Wear old clothes and be prepared to get down with the adult dogs and interact with them. Remember that puppies are cute, but it is an adult dog which you will live with for many years. Do not expect to simply sit on the sidelines and watch if you want to learn about the breed. A Dalmatian is often unsure of strangers. If you want to know the dog and the breed, you must be willing to make friends before you judge. Often breeders will not sell to people who come in good clothes and pick dog hair off their pants throughout the entire visit!

Do not expect to handle a litter of puppies, even if you are ready to buy. Many diseases are transmittable through handling, and the breeder has no way of knowing what you have been exposed to and may be carrying in terms of dog diseases. A breeder may ask you to only look at the puppies, not to touch them. Breeders do not have the kind of inflated prices, nor the callousness, which would allow them to simply write off the death of a puppy from over-handling, or being exposed to something a visitor may unknowingly be carrying.

Never visit more than one breeder on the same day. Not only is this often confusing, but it greatly increases the probability that you may carry germs from one kennel to another. Be considerate.

Do not expect to view a litter shortly after birth. Most breeders will limit viewing to puppies which have been weaned and are ready to go home. While it is a good idea to see the dam and the sire if possible, so that you have a good idea of what the puppy may grow up to look like, strangers around very young litters (under five weeks) may irritate the bitch, and unless you are very familiar with the bloodline, you will probably not be able to see anything more than a cute lump!

Finally, breeders often begin to sell their pups at or shortly before birth. Don't expect to get the "pick of the litter" if you wait until the puppies are born and ready to go home. In the first place, there is no single pick of the litter. Different puppies are best for different homes. A breeder who is really doing his job listens carefully to what each buyer is looking for and matches the puppy to the home. If the litter has, for example, five pups, one or all of them may be sold before they are eight weeks old. You may go to the kennel and fall in love with a puppy only to find it has been sold to someone who put their faith in the breeder at or around the time the litter was born. Different breeders handle this differently, but don't be surprised to find that if you want to see the litter before you buy, all or most of the pups may be sold before you get a chance to see them.

WHAT A BREEDER MAY ASK YOU

Besides questions about your household, most breeders will want to know if you have any plans for training, exercise and socialization. They will make recommendations based on what they believe are the needs of their dogs. They may ask if you intend to spay or neuter the puppy and at what age. They will ask you about other animals in your home, and what experience you have had with dogs in the past. They will want to know if your yard is fenced, what kind of living pattern you have and who comes in and out of the house on a regular basis. They will want to know about ages of children in the home and those who visit frequently. They will ask about the primary caretaker for the dog. They may want to know what your work schedule is and even if you are planning a family. *Don't look at these questions as an invasion of privacy. The breeder is trying to determine if the breed, the bloodline and the puppy are right for you and your home.* Almost every reputable breeder we talked to said that there had been people they simply refused to sell to because they did not think the dog, or in some cases even the breed, was the right fit. Through their years of labor and experience, breeders are trying to save you time, money and emotional problems by getting the right dog into the right home.

Dalmatians need lots of exercise, even in bad weather and a breeder will probably insist that you have a fenced yard and a place for the dog to play.

A breeder may ask that you have the puppy checked by your local veterinarian so that everyone can feel confident about the health of the puppy. (Do not expect most veterinarians to be experts on the finer points of conformation.)

One of the most important reasons for buying from a reputable breeder is his knowledge. It allows the breeder to match you with a puppy who will fit your needs, and it gives you support to fall back upon if you have problems. You become part of the extended family of the dog and have help on hand to get through the problems which may come up. Many a long time friendship has begun with a sale of a puppy.

WHAT A BREEDER SHOULD OFFER

Look for a breeder who is enthusiastic in talking about his dogs. A good breeder has put a lot of time and money into his breeding program. It is natural that he will talk freely and with knowledge about the pedigree, the individuals they own, and about the breed in general.

A breeder should offer a kennel pedigree of the dog. AKC will provide a certified copy of the actual pedigree for a fee, but breeders will usually give at least a handwritten copy with the puppy. This copy is not a certified pedigree, but should be accurate based on the breeder's kennel records. Champions should be marked, and sometimes other information such as color or BAER/BAEP (see chapter on health) certification is provided. There should be a fair number of titled dogs in the last three generations to ensure that the breeder has not gone too far from the standard and is still producing a dog which looks and acts like a good Dalmatian.

A breeder should offer some kind of proof that the breeding stock is free of hereditary diseases and/or some guarantee if the puppy does not turn out to be free of such problems. In Dalmatians, breeding stock should be BAER/BAEP hearing tested, and litters should be tested. However, don't expect more than you buy. A breeder may offer a guarantee for genetic defects which will affect the use of the dog as it is purchased. If a dog is purchased as a show and/or breeding dog, and only one testicle descends for example, this would make the dog ineligible to show, and basically unbreedable (dogs with one testicle can reproduce, but it is a fault which will be passed on to the offspring and therefore the dog SHOULD NOT be bred). A guarantee of replacement or some kind of refund, depending on the breeder, should certainly apply since the dog could not fulfill the original purpose for which he was purchased. If the dog was sold as a pet, there would be no guarantee for the problem since it does not affect in any way the dog's general health or ability to be a companion. Most breeders advise neutering pets, and therefore the single testicle would make no difference.

A breeder should give you a record of the shots and worming that the puppy has had. Puppies should not leave a breeder without at least one set of shots, and most breeders automatically worm puppies. Puppies, like babies, put everything in their mouths so it is very easy for them to pick up parasites.

A breeder should offer instructions on what to feed the pup and how to care for it.

Remember that no breeder is infallible. Even with the best of care and knowledge, a puppy may have a health or temperament problem. Breeders will usually not refund money, but many breeders will work with you to replace or exchange a puppy with a problem. Guarantees are usually less broad on an adult dog because health, temperament and conformation problems are easy to identify.

One legitimate reason many breeders do not give money back is because this would make the dog more of an investment for the new owner than a member of the family. If breeders were to offer money back, they would be functioning as a savings bank, allowing the dog to be returned for the purchase price any time the new owner felt they no longer wanted the dog, or any time they needed money. There is often a *lot* of difference in opinion about *how much* a partial refund should be, *how bad* the problem really is and *what part* of the blame is rightfully that of the breeder and what part is rightfully the blame of the owner. For all of these reasons, breeders usually prefer their dogs to go into homes where they will be appreciated and loved as members of the family. If the purpose of the buyer is truly to own a nice dog, then a replacement is the logical solution, still giving the owner what he wanted in the first place — a loving, healthy pet.

A breeder will probably ask you to call and let him know how the puppy is doing, how it is getting along in the new home and what it grows up to be. Remember, sending photos of the dog in his new home and again when he is an adult is a very nice way of saying "thank you" to your breeder. Like proud parents, most breeders want to know what happens to their pups, and what kind of adults they turn out to be. It is also a way for him to check how well their breeding program is working. Most of our breeders say they wish people would remember to do this. A photo at Christmas, on the dog's birthday, or any time you have an extra copy, is a wonderful present to any breeder truly interested in his dogs.

You should get a written contract detailing what you should get from the breeder and what he has a right to expect from you. It should include both the full registered name of the sire and dam, and their "call" names (nicknames). At least the call name should match what the dam has been called during your visit, and she should respond to it. It should state the full price and terms of the purchase, the date of birth for the pup, the sex of the pup, and the name of the breeder and owners. (They may be different.) This is a major purchase and rarely do two individuals recall all particulars precisely in the same way. A written contract protects both buyer and seller and should offer something to each of them.

HEALTH

*H*ereditary problems are a fact of life with almost all dogs — even mutts. Again, the reason to buy a pedigreed dog from a good breeder is that you have some idea of what kinds of health problems you may face, and how likely they are to show up in an individual animal. To think that there will be no health problems in any dog you buy is like thinking you will raise a child without ever having to take him to the doctor. By looking at the problems that are commonly found in the breed, learning how frequent they are and deciding if you can cope with them as they arise, you will be prepared for what you may encounter before you buy a puppy.

Learn what health problems are most frequent in the breed, and ask appropriate questions. Fortunately, eye problems (such as PRA — Progressive Retinal Atrophy) are seldom found in Dalmatians. Asking for a CERF (an eye test) number on Dalmatian breeding stock for example, would not be an appropriate question, although it would be a good question to ask for a Cocker Spaniel or Labrador Retriever.

DEAFNESS — One of the most talked about problems with the Dalmatian is deafness. The Dalmatian Club of America has issued a policy statement on deaf puppies, asking that they be put down. This call to owners, breeders and veterinarians is made for a number of reasons. First, the DCA is concerned that with the rising popularity of the breed, deaf, or even unilaterally (hears in one ear) deaf, Dalmatians may be bred. If you own a unilaterally deaf dog, ***Do Not Breed It.***

Bilaterally deaf dogs should not be taken into the home for a variety of reasons. First, as mentioned in a previous chapter, the condition involves more than simply the inability to hear. All pups of all breeds are born with their eyes and ears sealed shut. These open as the puppy matures, usually in a week to ten days and in some breeds as late as two weeks. With Dalmatians, at about four to six weeks, affected puppies will go deaf due to a degeneration of the neurons in the ear. Some studies indicate that this degeneration continues as the dog gets older and involves degeneration in the neurons of the brain. Behavior is apt to be or become erratic and frequently involves fear biting, aggression or other erratic behavior such as howling. In addition, death or injury because the dog cannot hear the owner's commands, because the dog may be hit by a car even in his own driveway, or because the dog cannot perceive danger is always a heartbreaking possibility.

Experienced, responsible breeders can test puppies for deafness and many breeders today have their litters BAER (Brainstem Auditory Evoked Response) or BAEP (Brainstem Auditory Evoked Potential) hearing tested where this service is available. This testing is just another reason why it is essential to purchase a Dalmatian puppy from a responsible breeder. BAER testing is done at five weeks of age, by a veterinarian in his office. Without this test, deaf puppies are not as easy to spot as would be expected because pups react as a group. A deaf pup will sometimes react to what he cannot hear because he copies his littermates. Unilaterally deaf pups are *very* difficult to identify except with a BAER test.

Deaf dogs are frequently difficult to control. An owner, kind hearted and meaning well, gives a deaf dog a home. Unable to manage the dog, but unable to live with it, the owner may place the dog in a new home instead of euthanizing it. That owner repeats the pattern, until the dog, already having difficulty coping with an environment he cannot hear, must adjust again and again to a new home, never finding a permanent, safe place.

The good news for Dalmatian buyers is that this is not a condition which develops late in life. Dogs will either be deaf from birth (or shortly thereafter), or they will have normal hearing throughout their lives.

Uric Acid and Stones — Dals possess a genetic characteristic unusual in dogs, yet common within the breed. The majority of Dals excrete a high level of uric acid in their urine compared to other canines. It is a curious fact that man, apes, the Dalmatian dog and certain species of rabbit phylogenetically have lost uricase activity. That is, they lack the ability to convert uric acid to more soluble allantoin within the liver cell. Dalmatians have therefore played a major role in certain types of research because of this condition.

Uric acid tends to form salts, such as ammonium urate. These salts may crystallize into stones, which in turn block the urethra and prevent elimination. Although the high level of uric acid is present in the majority of the breed, only about 2-5% (according to various estimates submitted by our breeders) will develop a problem. Bitches can develop stones, but blockage is far more frequent in males because of the narrower urinary tract through the penis. These stones are usually small, and the female can pass them out of the body without a problem in most cases. Although many vets will recommend operating immediately, and some will indicate that neutering is necessary, call your breeder before making a decision about surgery. Because of the low incidence of the problem in the general dog population, many vets are not well versed in more conservative remedies. There are alternative methods of treatment which might be appropriate to explore, and your breeder should be able to provide you with some guidance. Neutering, while always a good idea for a pet, may not be necessary. Daily medication of Allopurinol for the remainder of the life of the dog is usually recommended.

Some interesting things to keep in mind are: Most problems develop in males, mid-to later in life. Most of these dogs have had no previous symptoms. Uric acid stones are among the most responsive stones to treatment in both man and animals. Complete uric acid stone dissolution is often the result of treatment of forced fluids and drug therapy. Surgical removal of these stones is well described in veterinary literature and is not considered a complex surgical procedure.

One necessary factor in managing high uric acid levels is to maintain a low protein diet. One breeder compares high protein dog food to a person eating only red meat every day, with a low vegetable intake to balance the diet. She points out that several hundred years ago, in the days of Henry VIII — when people who could afford to often ate meat as an almost exclusive diet — gout was a common complaint. Likewise, Dals need to be maintained on a well balanced dog food of about 23% protein once they are full-grown. (Some breeders recommend feeding a diet as low as 20-21%, or as high as 26%, but 23% was the level most often mentioned. All agreed that high protein, or *"hot"* dog foods, should be avoided.)

Fluid intake is also a factor. Since stones cannot form in dilute urine, a dog whose intake of at least one quart (preferably one and a half to two quarts) of water per day would have a greatly reduced chance of forming stones. Milk or other additives can be used in order to entice the animal to drink fluids of this quantity.

Go out into the yard on occasion and watch your dog eliminate. This lets you know if he is having difficulty. He should produce a steady stream of a light straw color. Watch out for cloudy, red, or dark colored urine, urine with a strong heavy smell, or attempts to urinate which do not produce more than a dribble or two. Always have fresh water available, and do not allow him to go long periods of time without being able to relieve himself.

Other breeders think the entire problem occurs so seldom that it is overblown.

They cite that many Dalmatians have done quite well with whatever their owners happened to feed them and suggest that special dietary consideration only be pursued for dogs with a history or heritage of stone problems. Be sure to ask the breeder about the level of occurrence in his bloodline.

Hypothyroidism — This condition is frequent in a number of different breeds, including Dalmatians, and occurs in adult dogs equally in males and females. It is caused by inadequate T3/T4 production, which is usually the result of either a dysfunctional thyroid gland or a dysfunctional pituitary. The latter may be the result of injury instead of hereditary predisposition. The reduction in basal metabolic rate results in a gain in body weight, which may vary from slight to marked obesity. Affected dogs are frequently less active and are often "heat seekers," as they have difficulty in maintaining normal body temperature. Excessive shivering may be observed in some dogs and skin frequently feels cool to the touch.

Most common in Dalmatians are skin symptoms. The thyroid hormone is important for maintaining normal skin and hair growth, oil gland production, and bacterial flora. Affected dogs may have thin, dry, lusterless coats with hairs that fall off easily. Advanced cases exhibit symmetrical hair loss, particularly in the neck, trunk and dorsal area. The skin itself may become dry, rough and scaly and occasionally overly pigmented. Changes in skin and hair coat occur in most areas of friction. There may be a thickening of the skin in some areas.

Most of our breeders report that diagnosis and daily medication result in prompt response, although severe skin problems might take a month or two to be completely eliminated. Medication must be maintained for the duration of the dog's life.

Skin Problems from Allergies — Many skin problems are caused by allergic reactions. Carpet and carpet cleaner may be the problem. Some dogs are allergic to various grasses and weeds which may be in your area. Even laundry detergent may cause an outbreak. Some of our breeders report food as a major problem, so dogs may respond to a hypoallergenic diet such as lamb and rice-based food. If food is the cause, three to four weeks on a different diet should bring some improvement. The pattern of hair loss is usually along the bottom of the dog, the legs and belly, the throat and along the tail. Allergic skin problems are among the most frustrating because they persist throughout the life of the dog. Dogs with allergies SHOULD NOT BE BRED.

By far the most common allergy however is flea allergy. For some reason, people often tend to deny that their dog has fleas, as if it is somehow a reflection on their home and care. In certain areas of the country, fleas are an ongoing battle, especially in the summer. Just because you don't see a flea, doesn't mean that they aren't there. Regular spraying of the house, the yard and the dog will keep the problem under control. Once a dog gets a flea bite, especially if he is allergic to them, an infection may begin. Scratching with a dirty paw may lead to a bacterial infection, and the moisture from licking the area may lead to a fungus infection. At that point, any single treatment will not help because you are really dealing with several problems at the same time. The easiest thing to do is to keep the fleas from irritating the dog to begin with (see the chapter on Care). If you see black specks on your dog, usually at the point of the shoulder, at the base of the tail or on the stomach or chest, he has a flea problem.

OTHER DISEASES

Other problems mentioned by some of our breeders becoming more common, include Idiopathic Epilepsy (involving seizures or convulsive episodes and Hip Dysplasia. The latter condition was not mentioned as a particular problem in the breed. Although some conscientious breeders will rate their dogs with OFA (see below), and others may X-ray the hips, the problem was not widespread enough in the breed to be noted as exceptional by any of our breeders. One breeder who did mention hip dysplasia says that it — like PRA which is found in many breeds — is seldom found in the Dalmatian.

The Orthopedic Foundation for Animals (OFA) keeps a registry for all breeds, and will evaluate X-rays of any dog over a year old. But in order to get an OFA number certifying the dog as free of dysplasia, a dog must be over two years of age.

GENETIC ISSUES

One common myth is that if you do not buy from a "Show Breeder" you will get a healthier dog. Nothing can be further from the truth. Genetic problems exist throughout the breed. A backyard breeder, or one who has not taken the time to educate himself and make carefully planned breedings, will certainly perpetuate the health problems into future generations. Breeders who study the bloodlines and put health as a priority will succeed in reducing the number of incidents of certain health problems, even if they cannot eliminate them completely. The fact that responsible breeders refuse to breed a dog or bitch who is known to exhibit or carry undesirable traits will slowly reduce the number of offspring exhibiting those problems. People who simply breed without knowledge and care do the breed a great disservice by perpetuating and increasing the number of health problems found. (See the chapter on breeding.)

Inbreeding and line breeding are often thought to cause health problems. This is not true in itself. These practices can also be your assurance that you will NOT have the problem.

An inbred dog, one with several close breedings such as sister to brother, father to daughter, dam to son, etc., will be likely to produce more puppies with recessive traits. Recessive traits need to be carried on both sides in order to exhibit themselves in the puppy. If the breeding is close, the same recessive traits may exist on both sides and are more likely to be manifested in the puppy. The same is true, though to a lesser extent, in line breeding, where lines are bred back and forth using similarly bred animals who may not be direct relatives in the first generation or two. The difference between line breeding and inbreeding is the NUMBER of animals used in the gene pool.

This pup has one dark eye and one blue eye. Although acceptable in the standard, some of our breeders say they try to avoid blue eyes.

If a line is free of health problems, line breeding and inbreeding ensure that the puppies will be clear because there is no way for a recessive, offending gene to enter the gene pool. This is the argument breeders use for not outcrossing (introducing a new bloodline which may carry an unwanted recessive gene). But if the gene pool carries an offending gene, line breeding and certainly inbreeding will increase the chances of it turning up. Because recessive genes are impossible to identify by looking at the dog, breeders often do test breeding of close relatives to see if the trait will show up. It is their way of "testing" their gene pool.

Although line breeding and inbreeding are part of the intricate study of genetics, and something breeders spend their lives learning about, it is sufficient to realize that the practice of line breeding and inbreeding is no better, and no worse, than the quality of the stock from which the line began. In itself, the practice does not mean that the puppies will be healthy or unhealthy, aggressive or calm, large or small. It simply means that whatever recessive genes are lurking under the surface, the tighter the breeding, the more likely they are to manifest themselves in the puppies.

PUPPY SHOTS

Your puppy will come to you with vaccinations. But be prepared that these days, with rapidly mutating virus strains, the pattern of vaccinations may be different than it was a number of years ago. A number of drug companies have come up with new vaccines designed to combat the mutating virus strains. Some breeders begin to vaccinate very early. Others wait until a few weeks later. Some believe in the new "Fort Dodge KF-11 shot." Others think it is nothing more than pharmaceutical company hype. Norden has a "First Dose" which is supposed to take effect in spite of the effect of the mother's immunity. This vaccine eliminates the middle puppy shot. Get a copy of the kind of shots and the dates the puppy has received them, and take them to a vet. If your vet comments about the shots, remember that vaccination schedules are becoming more controversial every year. Our advice is to find a vet you feel comfortable with and fall in line with whatever he suggests. The fact is that puppies survive and prosper under a number of different programs; the important thing is to be sure that vaccinations are given. No harm is done if several types of shots are mixed during the lifetime of the pup.

Dalmatian pups are born white but will have some of their spotting by the time they are ready to go to their new homes.

Traditionally, puppies were given a vaccination at eight weeks, twelve weeks and sixteen weeks. Today, many breeders are beginning shots at five or six weeks. The vaccines contained in combination shots are different today than they were ten or twenty years ago. Many breeders and vets are no longer vaccinating against leptospirosis, but several new vaccines have come into use and are changing each year. How many vaccinations, what vaccines are contained in a combination shot, or if a combination shot is given, and how frequently these shots are given will vary from breeder to breeder, and even from veterinarian to veterinarian. It is safe to say you should NEVER take home a puppy that has not had at least the first in the series of vaccinations. Remember, no matter what the breeder has done about vaccinations, the final vaccination will be needed AFTER four months of age.

The traditional three vaccinations are not given because the puppy needs three doses to build up immunity, but because the immunity that the puppy received from the dam slowly decreases. The antibodies he was born with will gradually wear off, but there is no way of knowing if this immunity will wear off at five weeks or sixteen weeks. A series of vaccinations is given so that the shortest time possible will elapse between the time the mother's immunity wears off and the time the puppy is given the next vaccination and develops immunity on his own. Four months is the outside time when the immunity could wear off, and therefore if a vaccination is given AFTER four months, it is sure to produce a mature immunity. This process is what is meant by a "maturing immune system."

Rabies vaccinations work much the same way, except that only the mature shot is given. Some states require that shot to be given at four months of age. Others are of the opinion that four months is too young, and they prefer to give the rabies vaccination after six months of age. Although DHLP and other vaccinations may be given by breeders, state laws require that rabies vaccinations be given by a vet.

All dogs should be vaccinated again at one year of age and every year after that for the rest of their lives. Rabies shots should be given according to state laws, which vary in the length of time a rabies vaccination will be considered "good."

Most of our breeders recommend that you do not expose the puppy to dogs outside the home until after the final puppy shot at four months of age. This means that he should not visit friends and relatives with dogs, and he should not go to public parks, walkways, or any other area with heavy dog traffic. Even after inoculation, the titer (immunity level in the blood) does not reach safe levels for approximately ten days after the vaccination.

Ask your local vet about Heartworm, Lyme Disease, and a worming program in your area of the country. Climate, weather conditions and geographic location make the incidence of these problems vary from one place to another. If you are buying a puppy from a warm, humid climate, the chances are that he may have worms. This is not a reflection on the breeder. Even with a conscientious worming program, breeders in the Southeast have more problems than those in the hot, dry areas of the Rocky Mountains or in cold northern climates.

SELECTING A VET

One of the most important things you can do is select a vet. Like doctors, not all vets are alike in their attitudes and treatment programs. Don't be alarmed if your breeder does not accept everything your vet may say about the puppy as the absolute truth. Veterinary medicine, just like human medicine, is not an exact science. Breeders have been working with the same genetic pool for many years; the vet comes into the room and sees the puppy for the first time, often without a strong background in either the breed or the bloodline. Beware of comments about the puppy other than those strictly related to health.

Although most vets are careful professionals, breeders have some recommendations in selecting a vet: If your vet, either with a previous dog or with your new dog, begins to suggest rare conditions and complicated health problems, get a second opinion. This is simply good practice, especially if treatments are costly. And don't get the second opinion from another vet in the same office. People who work together often take the same approach to a problem. This makes for good working conditions, but it does not give a true second opinion.

A healthy, happy, well behaved Dalmatian is a joy to his owner.

Secondly, if your vet begins to make wide sweeping generalizations about the breed and your dog — especially on the first visit — think twice about what he is saying. Most vets are not experts in specific breeds and often see a far greater number of health problems (because they see unhealthy dogs much more often than the once a year they see a healthy dog), and may base their opinion of the breed on a few problem individuals.

As an owner, it is your job to be sure your dog is sufficiently socialized and trained so there will not be a problem controlling him on visits to the vet.

HOLISTIC MEDICINE AS AN ALTERNATIVE

Recently, people have become very interested in natural healing alternatives commonly referred to as "holistic," "complementary" or "alternative" medicines. Acupuncture, chiropractic, nutrition, herbs and homeopathy are the most widespread alternative therapies available. This interest is expanding rapidly into the world of pets. Conventional medicine follows a reductionist philosophy, focusing on what is considered the exact location or cause of disease and attempting to remove it, kill it or suppress it. For example, tumors are removed or destroyed, antibiotics are used to kill germs and allergic reactions are suppressed with drugs.

Practitioners of holistic or alternative medicines feel the problem is that none of these therapies address the real reasons the pet is sick. Healthy animals do not get serious infections, tumors or allergies. A pet's immune system is malfunctioning BEFORE these "diseases" occur. Therefore, what needs to be addressed is the functioning of the ENTIRE body, mind and spirit of the pet. Through this approach, the whole body functions better and can prevent or cure almost anything, according to those who practice holistic medicine.

A wide variety of holistic remedies have been used on Dalmatians to varying degrees of success. There are a number of breeders and owners who believe the health of their pets has been improved with such practices.

Vaccination has become a focus for some practitioners of holistic medicine. Noting that some Dalmatian puppies develop the diseases for which they have recently been inoculated, some believe that elimination of such vaccinations is an alternative. Other breeders prefer to space out their vaccinations, or not to give them in combinations. Some breeders believe that annual boosters are not necessary, especially for dogs with other medical problems. The serious followers of holistic medicine feel that good nutrition and homeopathy can prevent these conditions as well if not better than vaccination. **IT IS IMPORTANT TO NOTE THAT SIMPLY FORGOING VACCINATIONS IS NOT THE ANSWER.** *If you are interested in holistic medicine, take the time to learn more about it and tailor it to your dog, his needs and your ability to provide the necessary program.* Holistic medicine as a prevention of disease is based on maintaining good health through a number of different applications, *all* of which must be carefully maintained in order for the program to work!

Nutrition - The wide variety of opinions on dog nutrition has often led to conflicting nutritional programs. Food preservatives have sometimes been blamed for allergic reactions. Others feel that pets suffer as a direct result of inadequate and even toxic pet foods. Still others feel that food must be fed as it is in nature — RAW and including organs and glands, bones, vegetables, live digestive bacteria and active enzymes. Almost all of these schools of thought hold that natural nutrition can improve virtually any condition and by itself cure a great many. Supplements, such as those mentioned in our Shopping Arcade section, have been found by some breeders to improve the quality of life, from improving temperament and energy levels to eliminating skin or immune problems. Allergic dermatitis has often been traced to foods.

Acupuncture - Acupuncture has been used for thousands of years. The life energy of the body (chi) flows through a series of channels (meridians). This energy is responsible for maintaining health and body functions. The energy may become excessive, deficient or blocked. There are points along the meridians through which the energy flow can be adjusted, usually through the use of needles. Lasers and pressure (acupressure) may also be used. Balancing and restoring energy flow can result in tremendous health benefits. With the improved health, diseases are eliminated.

Chiropractic - The central nervous system is a major communications system within the body. Interference with nerve function can result in a tremendous number of symptoms. Physical and emotional stresses cause misalignment of spinal bones and impeded nerve communication. Chiropractic adjustments restore proper nervous system function, resulting in the elimination of a variety of health problems. There is another benefit to chiropractic that is not often discussed. Three acupuncture meridians (see above) run along and beside the spinal bones. Therefore, realigning the spine allows better energy flow.

Herbs - There are different systems of herbal medicine in use: Chinese, Western and Ayurvedic (from India). The Chinese and Ayurvedic approaches focus on the energy of the body. Different herbs are used to balance the body. The Chinese system attempts to balance Yin and Yang, the opposite types of energy within the body. If the body is too Yin, the herbalist balances it with Yang herbs and vice versa. There are also herbs to strengthen the life energy (chi) and cleanse and nourish the body. Western herbs focus more on the physical body. The herbs nourish and/or cleanse the body, thereby strengthening its ability to heal.

Homeopathy - Homeopathy is a system of medicine which is nearly 200 years old. According to the law of similars, disease is cured by stimulating the body with an energy remedy. The remedy is derived from a substance which, if given in large doses, is capable of producing the same symptoms the patient is experiencing. For example, homeopathically prepared onion (allium cepa) may be given if a patient is experiencing tearing eyes, watery, irritating discharge from the nose and a desire for fresh air. Most of you would recognize these symptoms as those produced when exposed to the vapors of cut onions. However, these symptoms may also occur in someone with hayfever. The cause is not important. How the individual responds is what counts. This results in individualized remedy selection based on the patient, NOT THE DISEASE. The treatment of arthritis in ten dogs may require a different remedy for each one.

These are only a few of the holistic alternatives available. Others include massage, Bach flower essences, bio-magnets, and scent and color therapy. The practitioners of all of these systems recognize the individual as a whole body with a mind and spirit, not as a liver or kidney problem. They realize that only the individual can heal him or herself. However, the healing mechanisms must be allowed to operate unhindered. Holistic healing methods maximize healing functions and remove existing impediments.

Other varieties of holistic medicine include a balance between holistic and conventional medicine. First aid, basic health care, nutritional balance and basic remedies based on vitamins, minerals, trace elements and herbs are used to keep the dog healthy, improve his immune system and prevent common ailments before they develop.

Some Dalmatians seem to do well with some of these treatments, but it is important to take the time to understand the process and to tailor it to your individual pet's needs.

BRINGING HOME A NEW DOG OR PUPPY

When you have selected your new dog, you need to get ready for its arrival. Decide who in the family is responsible for the care, feeding, exercise and discipline of the dog. Decide what rules the dog and the members of the family must live by. Dalmatians adapt to a routine. They will expect that one member must arrive home before they can go on their walk. They may learn that when they see a certain pattern of behavior it means an outing which will include them, while another pattern of behavior means that the family will leave, and they will stay at home. They will learn sounds of cars which belong in the family, and who is a regular visitor. They will learn where and how to go out to the bathroom, and when food will be provided. It is good to decide on a pattern of care before the dog or puppy arrives.

If you have purchased your dog before it is ready to go home, sometimes a breeder will furnish you with a list of things you will need to have on hand when the dog arrives home. If you have not been provided with such a list, ask for one. It should include the feeding schedule and the type of food the breeder has been feeding.

An adult Dalmatian will eat from three to five cups of dog food per day, depending on the brand and the individual metabolism of the dog. Puppies eat smaller quantities more often, but because they are growing, they will eat more than you would expect if you simply calculate the weight of the pup in relation to his full grown size. A puppy must be fed three or four times a day, depending on his age and established patterns. This schedule can gradually be reduced to twice a day by the time he is six months old, and once for an adult. Puppies do well on high quality commercial puppy foods, which are formulated for the pup's rapid growth and activity. Adults generally do best on a lower-protein food. Stay away from foods labeled "high stress" or "high protein" unless your dog is very active, such as doing road trial training. There is more discussion on foods in the chapters on health and care.

Your pup should be bright-eyed. His coat should be shiny and his feet a little too big for him. Expect him to be uncoordinated and interested in everything around him. He will grow rapidly and outgrow his collar, his bed, and perhaps even his bowl, so keep that in mind when you make your early purchases. Select a vet (see health chapter) if you do not have one already and be sure he is familiar with Dalmatians and likes the breed. Take the pup to the vet as soon as possible after you pick him up. Give the veterinarian the vaccination information and let him look over the pup and set up a schedule for additional shots and regu-

lar checkups. Most good breeders strongly recommend this kind of veterinary check up so that everyone can feel good about the health of the dog when it arrives at the new home.

He should be at least eight weeks old according to most of our breeders, although a few say seven weeks is all right. Puppies need that time with their litter to socialize. During the early weeks of life, the mother teaches them discipline by rolling them over or bumping them with her nose when they get out of hand. After they are weaned, which is generally about five or six weeks, pups will learn social skills from their littermates. A puppy which is older than twelve weeks and still with the litter should have had ample time alone with a human so that he has bonded and been influenced by humans rather than the pack of pups he lives with. If you cannot pick up your puppy until he is older, be sure to talk to your breeder about how he plans to handle this more advanced socialization. By airline regulations, a puppy flying to his new home must be at least eight weeks old.

Before you bring the new dog or puppy home, be prepared. Get food and water bowls of appropriate size, and decide where to put them. They should be heavy enough that he cannot tip them over or push them across the floor while eating or drinking. Bowls with bottoms almost as large as their tops are better than bowls, such as human serving bowls, which have a smaller circumference at the bottom than at the top. Such bowls tip over easily.

Dalmatians shed and need to be groomed to keep the hair problem under control. When your pup arrives, you should be prepared to begin getting him used to grooming from the time he is young. Have on hand a bristle brush, a rubber curry or a horsehair mitt which seem to be best for getting dead hair off the Dalmatian's short coat. You will also need toenail clippers or grinders so you can keep the feet trimmed. See more about grooming in the chapter on care.

Decide where the dog will sleep. If you are using a crate, be sure it will fit if it needs to stay up most of the time. It must be somewhere where it will be out of the way of the family and the family should understand that the bed or crate is "off limits." Pups need to sleep frequently and they need a place where they can get away and relax. A bed or blanket may be good indoors, while outside, a box with shavings may be better. A bored Dalmatian will almost certainly drag a blanket or pillow all over the yard, and may even reduce the large blanket to several small ones!

Plan a well-balanced exercise pattern for the dog. He will need enough time to run off his energy, With too much time alone, he may begin his own landscaping project or turn the garden hose into a "soaker."

When the dog is in the house, he usually uses his "house manners" and will be more willing to appreciate his bed, pillow or blanket and leave it in one piece. However, don't leave him alone for long periods of time until he is older and more mature or you are likely to find he has made some alterations of his own to cabinets and furniture.

Toys or chew bones are good things to have on hand, but they should be large in size. The rawhide chew bones with a knot on the end are preferred by breeders over the flat chips, which be-

Have chew toys on hand. They help save the house by giving the pup something of his own to chew.

come soft and may choke a dog if swallowed. There are a number of good chew items on the market today including preserved pig's ears and cattle hooves. These have a lot of appeal to Dalmatians as do a wide variety of toys. One breeder recommends an empty plastic milk carton as a good toy, light enough to pop and be thrown about and large enough that it cannot be swallowed. These make great noise and dogs love them. But since they can easily be chewed up they should be removed when the dog tires of them and begins to settle in to serious demolition.

Most of our breeders caution against leaving a collar on a dog, especially a puppy. Small feet may get hung up in it, or it may become hooked on something in the house or yard. Put the collar on when you are taking him on the leash, and remove it before you leave him unattended, even in the crate. Puppies will sometimes need to wear a collar so that they can get used to the feel. It can be a real disaster to leave this introduction to the day obedience classes begin when he is six or eight months old! Either put the collar on him when you are around to watch, or use a buckle-on collar that is the proper size, not too small as to be uncomfortable, but not large enough to get a foot caught. A buckle-on collar should be loose enough to slip one finger easily between the collar and his neck. If you can slip more than two fingers in the collar easily, it is too loose. *Never leave him unattended with a slip, or "choke" collar.*

Arrange to pick up your dog or pup at a time when you will be home. Friday may be good, if you have time on the weekend to spend with him and help him get used to you as a new owner. On the first night home, whether you have picked up the pup or had him flown in, be prepared for him to be lonely, especially when the lights are turned out. It is likely that he has never been away from his littermates and he will probably cry or carry on. Be firm but understanding. Most of our breeders feel that the best way to handle a howling puppy was to simply ignore him. He will carry on for a night or two, but without any response from the human family he will soon adapt to the fact that night time is for sleeping. Soon, he will quietly join in the routine. If you continue to get up and try to comfort him, he will learn that the howling and sharp puppy yelping will bring human attention and comfort and once learned, he will be very reluctant to give up the behavior.

Keep pups contained when you are not watching them to help prevent them from developing bad habits which may be hard to cure later.

Establish a routine from the beginning. Discuss ahead of time with your breeder or family how you intend to handle this. Will you put the crate in your bedroom? Will you simply let him quiet himself? Where will you put him if you are not using a crate?

Dalmatians are good watch dogs and are usually not idle barkers. They will favor the person who cares for them, plays with them and feeds them, especially if it is the same person who does all three. However, when the jobs are taken over by another person, they will switch favorites. Dalmatians do love to play and get human attention, and they will be loving toward the entire family if everyone is involved with them at some level.

If you purchase an older dog, be aware that although the dog may be housetrained in his old surroundings, it may take several days or even weeks to adjust to the new family and new surroundings. Let him have time to adjust before you overwhelm him. Be kind, yet firm in the rules. It is kinder to establish what you expect of him from the beginning than to let him adjust and then to impose rules once he has become comfortable. Once he adjusts, the older dog will be ready to join right in with the new family, to travel and meet friends, to play with preteen or teenage children. He does not require as much time, training or care as a puppy.

Be prepared with a dog bed which is located somewhere out of the traffic pattern of the human family members.

Most of our breeders strongly recommend using a crate to housetrain, and to establish a pattern with either an older dog or a puppy. Contrary to some popular opinion, many dogs love crates. A crate is their cave, their home. Dogs, like their ancestors the fox, wolf and coyote, like the feeling of a "den," and the most successful doghouses are not huge structures, but small, enclosed areas that allow for "nesting." If you are buying a crate, be sure to get one big enough for the dog to live in as an adult, but not too big. One which is too large allows the puppy to soil it, and one which is too small is uncomfortable. Most breeders recommend what is commonly known as a #400 crate; ask your breeder for the exact size. Wire or plastic airline crates are both good.

Crating not only helps housetrain, it also allows the owner to relax and enjoy himself without worrying about the dog, watching it to be sure it does not soil the carpet, or keeping an eye out to see if it is tearing up the house. *Use the crate with common sense. Never leave a dog in a crate for excessive lengths of time.* Dalmatian pups are like two-or three-year-old children. They are curious and into just about everything. They need constant supervision when out of their crates and allowed to be with the family, and they need firm discipline from the beginning, enforcing consistent rules of behavior for the household.

Ask your breeder if the pup or dog is crate trained. Many breeders are believers in crates, and all show dogs must learn to travel and stay in crates at dog shows. If the dog is an older dog who has shown, he will probably be crate trained already. If the dog is not trained, put him in the crate and leave the room, staying near the door. He will probably sit there for a few minutes, then begin to cry, whine, scratch or bark. At the first noise, intervene with a sharp "NO!" The dog or puppy will begin to associate the startling voice with his attempts to get out of the crate. Some of our breeders suggest using a water pistol or spray bottle filled with clear water. When the dog or pup begins to cry, shoot a sharp, short burst of water at the dog until he stops. Repeating this several times with the word "NO!" seems to make the point a little more strongly. (They also suggest using a water gun when the dog was out of the crate to stop unwanted behavior in the house, such as chewing or scratching at doors.)

Once he is quiet in the crate for about thirty to forty-five minutes, praise him quietly. Don't make a big thing out of this. Put him outside. If you are housetraining him and he goes to the bathroom when you put him out, praise him lavishly.

Bring him back in the house and let him play and be free for fifteen to twenty minutes. If he begins to chew something that is not a toy, take it away, say "No!" sharply, and replace the item with one of his toys. Dalmatians love toys and can easily be distracted with them. After play time, put him back in the crate and repeat the process. Consistency will help him learn housetraining through association. He should be crate trained after only a few short tries. Other lessons may take longer!

He should be able to keep the crate clean all night by the time he is three to four months old. The more careful you are with your routine, and the more consistent, the more rapidly he will train. If you allow *either a new adult or a puppy* to have "accidents" in the house, you will have an even harder time breaking him of the habit later on. Never let him out of your sight until you are sure you can trust his judgment. Never give him more time to play and be free in the house than he can handle without having an accident. By the time he is four or five months old, he should be fairly well house trained. The fewer times he makes a mistake, the sooner he will be a reliable member of the family. ***Use common sense and remember not to leave him in the crate too much.***

Puppies are like babies. A puppy will need time to grow up and he will take much more than a couple of weeks to be housetrained. He will chew, may dig, and will carry things around. Dalmatians mature slowly, especially mentally. It will still take him several years to grow up and be mature. Like a baby, it simply takes him time to get rid of some of his exuberant puppy energy, learn manners and behave like a companion should behave. Judgment on what is his and what is yours, how to please you, and how to use his energy will take time and maturity. Don't become discouraged or angry with him. It is simply a

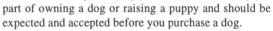

part of owning a dog or raising a puppy and should be expected and accepted before you purchase a dog.

Because puppies are so much fun, friends and family members may be tempted to overpower a puppy and exhaust him, lowering his resistance. Give the pup time to get adjusted to his new environment. Do not allow friends and family to carry him around to the point of exhaustion.

If you have a dog already, be aware that your older dog may dominate your new puppy. Do not allow your new puppy to be kenneled or fed with an older dog. The puppy could be permanently ruined by a strong-willed dog. No matter how kind the older dog may seem, he may dominate the younger dog.

Your expectations should be consistent and should never encourage behavior in a pup that you cannot accept in an older dog. For example, if you do not want an older dog on the sofa, don't pull a pup up on the couch with you. If you do not want a hundred pound dog jumping on you, don't let a pup jump. It may be cute when little puppy paws reach your knee, but it is not so much fun when a grown Dalmatian puts his paws on your chest. Another common example, a pup may stare at you, then if you hold his stare, snap at your face. This is funny with an uncoordinated puppy, but not funny at all in an adult dog. If you do not think the behavior is appropriate for an adult dog, DO NOT LET THE PUPPY BEGIN THE BEHAVIOR. Correct him sharply with a "NO" when he starts it. It is much harder to break bad habits than to establish the ground rules at the beginning.

Feeding schedules should find a routine which is convenient for both you and the dog, but which is consistent from day to day to promote housetraining. Remember, it takes six hours for food to go through a dog. Feed him and walk him or let him out for exercise on a regular basis. Regular exercise in the form of walks or playtime will also help regulate his system. Always let him out the last thing before you leave the house and the last thing at night. After a while he will get used to the routine and realize this is his last chance to go to the bathroom before having to spend time in his crate. This routine will help encourage him to eliminate and reduce the likelihood of soiling his crate.

TRAINING A DOG YOU CAN LIVE WITH!

Good training and exercise seem to be the hardest things for pet owners to understand and give their dogs. Our breeders recommend obedience classes. Dalmatians are very good in obedience work in the ring, but even if you never intend to show, obedience classes help you raise a well mannered dog you can live with. Early training is very important. Without it, a problem dog can develop and **problem dogs are the ones who end up in the SPCA**. No breeder wants to think of his or her puppy ending up in a rescue situation. Breeders say over and over again that proper socialization — that is, exposing the dog to strangers and a wide variety of situations as well as spending quality, loving time with him at home — is the most important thing and insures success. One breeder says that how long it takes to housetrain and leash train, and whether a Dalmatian is neurotic as an adult, all depended on the consistency and care of early training and socialization. **Time invested in a puppy is invaluable in producing a good dog,** and lack of time invested in a puppy is very difficult to make up once the dog is an adult with bad habits or a neurotic personality.

Decide what the dog will be allowed to do and be consistent. Don't let a puppy sleep on the bed or sofa unless you want to allow the adult to sleep on the bed.

If you have children in your home, have a long discussion with them on care and treatment of the dog *before you buy*. Children need to respect the dog as a living thing. Even toddlers can learn to treat a dog gently and not abuse it by kicking, slapping or pulling its tail. *If a baby is old enough to crawl, he is old enough to learn the word "no," just as a puppy does and he can learn not to tease the dog*. Puppies and babies are on about the same mental level and it is necessary that they are both taught respect from the very beginning. Older children need to be taught that Dalmatian pups may *look* like the stuffed toys produced after the movie, but they need to be treated very differently. Gentleness is a **must**.

There are several good books and videos on training. If there are no obedience classes in your area, buy one or two of these publications or a video on the subject, and read or view it thoroughly. Puppies are cute but some cute puppy behaviors are NOT cute in an adult.

KEEP IN TOUCH WITH THE BREEDER

A good breeder's job does not stop when the puppy goes home. Call the breeder when you arrive home or when the dog arrives by plane to let him know that everything is fine. Call him in a few weeks and discuss any problems or rewarding experiences you have had with your new family member. Send a photo whenever you can. This feedback helps breeders evaluate their breeding programs, and most of them truly enjoy hearing news of their "children."

Sometimes, due to changes in lifestyle or family pattern, it becomes necessary to find a new home for the dog. If so, you should contact the breeder BEFORE you give the dog away to a new home or take him to the SPCA. Many breeders require this notice in their contracts, but we suggest that you make the effort to contact the breeder under such circumstances whether it is mentioned in your contract or not. Good breeders are interested in their dogs, and they wish to follow them throughout their lifetime.

PAPERWORK

*T*he term "AKC registered" has meant, up until a few years ago, that a dog simply had a dam which carried AKC papers and a sire which carried AKC papers and they were both of the same breed. Any dog with two registered parents was eligible for registration, regardless of its quality.

In recent years, AKC has responded to pressure to put some limit to the number of breeding dogs in the general population. Since 1991, dogs may be marked by their original breeder as "non-breedable." This designation means that the dog will be issued papers from the AKC with a gold, rather than a purple, border. If such an animal is bred, even if bred to a dog or bitch with a regular purple bordered certificate with full breeding privileges, the puppies produced will not be eligible for registration with AKC.

The registered name of a dog is often in two or three parts. The kennel name of the original breeder usually begins the name, followed by the name of the individual dog, and finally a second kennel name may precede or follow if the dog was purchased as an unnamed puppy by another breeding kennel. This practice dates back to the early years in England and Europe when dogs were referred to by their owner's name first, because names in those days were very simple and duplication of names for dogs in the field was common. To make reference easier, people began to refer to the dogs as "Lord Grimstone's Susan" or "the Duke of Hamilton's Sam." These, combined with the year of their whelping, comprised the early pedigree records.

Today, a dog may be named, as with the bitch on page 85, "Ch. Driftwood Rambler She's A Ten, CDX," nicknamed "Button." The name shows that the dog named "She's A Ten" was bred by Rambler Dalmatians, owned by Joanne & Jim Nash — the Ch. before the name designates that she has earned her championship title — and was purchased as a puppy (before registration) by Kathryn Blink of Driftwood Farm Dalmatians. She has also earned a second level obedience title, CDX which follows the name. Thus the dog is "Ch. (the championship title earned through dog shows) Driftwood (the owner) Rambler (the breeder) She's A Ten (the name of the individual dog) CDX (obedience title).

Dogs bred and owned by a breeder at the time of registration will carry only one kennel name, usually in front of the individual dog's name. The dog on page 67, "Ch. Chalkhills Felony," was bred by Patricia Wallace-Jones and J.R. Jones of Chalkhills Dalmatians. The dog's name is "Felony." She was owned by Chalkhills Dalmatians at the time of her registration, and was still owned by them at the time of printing. Sometimes the kennel name will follow the name of the dog as on page 86, "Ch. Razzou of Robinwood." "Razzou" is the name of the dog and "Robinwood" is the name of the kennel owned by John and Sara Ledgerwood.

Sometimes the call name for the dog has nothing at all to do with the dog's registered name. On page 68, Am/Can Ch. Deluxe High Fashion Dots, CGC, is not called "Dot," as might be expected, but "Gucci." (The "Am/Can" which precedes the name indicates that Gucci has earned conformation titles in both the United States and in Canada.) Her son, Deluxe Dynamite Extrodinair, is called "Ike." Likewise, on page 69, Am/Can Ch. Proctor's Dappled Hi-Flyer is called "Maverick." If you talk to a breeder about the sire and dam of your pup, it is possible that the names they use when discussing the litter with you will not be the same as the names which show up on the papers later. If you think this may bother you, be sure to ask the registered name right from the start so you can keep it straight.

The titles CD, CDX, UD, CGC, RD, RDX and TT are working titles which are earned and stay throughout the life of the dog. Working titles follow the name and are explained more fully at the beginning of the Hall of Fame section. Ch. Dapper-Dan's Pongo, UD (page 75) has the highest obedience title which can be earned, and on page 76, Am/Can Ch. Belle Aire's Star E Knight, CGC, RD, has earned the title Canine Good Citizen and a Road Trial title. This is a new title offered only to Dalmatians. There is more about this competition and other working titles in the chapter on Dog Shows and Other Competitions.

Ch. Centennial Doctor Pepper (page 80) was purchased by Peter Capell who owns Dals of Doctor Pepper. He purchased the pup from Centennial Dalmatians, who were the breeders and owned the dam. Their kennel name, Centennial and Peter's kennel name (Doctor Pepper) make up the entire name for the dog. Another interesting way to handle kennel names is Ch. Folklore 'N' Firesprite Wm Tell on page 89. He was born from a bitch owned by Norma Baley of Firesprite Dalmatians and was sold on a co-ownership to Robert and Diana Skibinski of Folklore Dalmatians. "Wm Tell," as the pup was named, carries the name of both kennels who own him — "Folklore 'N' Firesprite." These are unusual ways to handle names, but there are no hard and fast rules.

When you buy a puppy, the breeder should give you a kennel pedigree. This will be a "tree" of names, like those in the "Hall of Fame" section. It lists the sire, dam, grandparents, and so on of the puppy. It will look something like this:

```
                                    grand sire of sire
                    sire of sire
                                    grand dam of sire
        sire
                                    grand sire of sire
                    dam of sire
                                    grand dam of sire
YOUR DOG
                                    grand sire of dam
                    sire of dam
                                    grand dam of dam
        dam
                                    grand sire of dam
                    dam of dam
                                    grand dam of dam
```

You should also receive either the AKC registration papers or more likely, the "AKC DOG REGISTRATION APPLICATION" shown below. The former is white, with a purple or gold border; the latter is a blue form and must be submitted to AKC to receive the registration certificate. When you buy a puppy, it is possible that a breeder may not

60 ✧ BASIC GUIDE TO THE DALMATIAN

even have the dog registration applications for the litter back from AKC, especially if the puppy is very young. But you should get some kind of kennel pedigree, and at least a note listing the sire, dam and date of whelping to assure you the puppy is registered.

If the breeder has the dog registration applications — commonly called "puppy registrations" — back from AKC, they will be on blue paper. THIS IS NOT YOUR REGISTRATION CERTIFICATE. Be sure this blue form is filled out completely. Ask your breeder about naming your puppy. Some breeders insist that pups be named with a certain letter of the alphabet to help them track their pups throughout the years. Sometimes

The BLUE litter registration will enable you to register your dog. Fill it out, including the name chosen for your dog, in the boxes provided. Fill in the color and the back of the form and send it to AKC for your dog's registration. THIS IS NOT YOUR REGISTRATION - AND YOU ONLY HAVE ONE YEAR FROM THE DATE THIS APPLICATION WAS ISSUED TO BE ABLE TO REGISTER YOUR DOG!

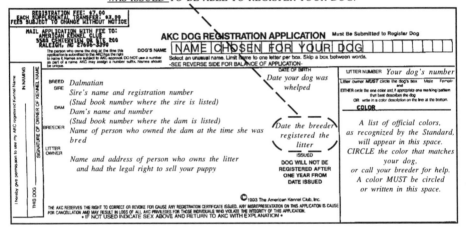

this can lead to funny and awkward names, especially if the letter is "X," "Y" or "Q!" Others will require that a word or idea be included in the name. Look to see which box is checked on the back of the form in regard to breedability of the dog. Be sure the breeder has signed as owner of the litter. Finally, be sure that "sex" and "color" are checked on the front of the puppy registration form.

ACCORDING TO AKC RULES which have only been in effect a few years, YOU MUST REGISTER THE DOG WITHIN ONE YEAR OF THE TIME THE PUPPY PAPERS HAVE BEEN ISSUED, or it cannot be registered. Therefore, it is important to take care of the paperwork as soon as possible.

Keep your kennel papers if you have them. If they were not provided, you can get a certified copy from AKC or use a pedigree service such as the one mentioned in the Shopping Arcade section. Canine Family Tree will provide you with a complete pedigree, usually faster and less expensively than AKC. If you intend to breed your dog, you will most certainly need to know what is "behind" him or her. You will need to make inquiries about the strengths and weaknesses of these ancestors, and what will be most likely to match up with your pedigree to produce good quality puppies. If you intend to hire your male out for stud, bitch owners will ask to see a copy of the pedigree. If you wish to take your bitch to a stud for breeding, most stud owners will ask to see the pedigree before they agree to use their stud. They will want to look for lines with known health problems, and lines that will or will not match with those of their stud.

PAPERWORK ✧ 61

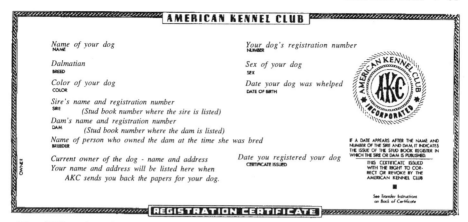

The AKC registration certificate for your dog will be issued when you fill out your blue puppy registration and submit it to AKC with the required fee, or, if you have an older dog, when you transfer your dog's registration to your name.

    Even if you never intend to breed, it is worth the investment to send to a pedigree service such as Canine Family Tree and get a copy. Champions of record will be marked in red, and it is a chance to see what famous dogs are in your dog's pedigree. You may enjoy matching the pedigree with those listed in the "Hall of Fame" section, looking for not only particular individuals, but familiar kennel names. When you receive your AKC registration certificate, it will NOT list the pedigree beyond the sire and dam of your dog. Send this information and their registration numbers (or simply send a photocopy of the registration certificate) to the pedigree service for the complete pedigree. The AKC registration is 8.5" X 4" with a purple or gold border and the official AKC incorporation seal. It will also list the current owner and breeder.

    If your dog is older and has already been registered, you will need to follow the "transfer instructions" on the back of the registration certificate. On the back, fill out Section A completely, be sure Section B has been signed and send in the fee and the ORIGINAL CERTIFICATE. AKC will issue a new certificate, with you listed on the front as the owner.

DOG SHOWS AND OTHER COMPETITIONS

*M*any a dog has lived his entire life as a companion, friend and confidant to his family without ever finding the need to have a career of his own. But some dogs do work for a living, and if they prove worthy, will earn a degree or title to attach to their names. The most common of these is a "Conformation" title from AKC. Conformation means "manner of formation; structure; form, as a physical entity" according to *Webster's Universal Unabridged Dictionary*. Simply stated, it is what the dog looks like standing still and moving at a trot, and how well he matches the written standard for the breed. As you can see from our Hall of Fame section, dogs of outstanding quality and attitude have earned the title "Champion." (Ch. appears before their registered name, and is used every time the registered name is printed.) Once earned, this title, like all dog titles, will stay with the dog forever. A champion is a champion for life.

Championships are earned by exhibiting at AKC shows and collecting points. The number of points earned at each show will vary, depending on the number of dogs of that breed which are entered in competition and defeated. It takes fifteen points for a dog to be a champion, but at least twice in his life the dog must win a "Major," that is, he must earn three points at one show. This feat is not as easy as it might seem, since there are not many majors a year, and the dog must win the top award in heavy competition.

Points are awarded for each breed based on how many dogs are showing in the area each year. There are nine AKC divisions across the country and the points may be different for each division and each breed within the division. Points may even be different for each sex within the same breed. For example, the chart below shows the points needed for six of the nine AKC divisions for shows held between May 1, 1996, and May 1, 1997. The Northeast includes: Connecticut, Maine, Massachusetts, New Hampshire, New York, Rhode Island and Vermont; the Southeast includes: Alabama, Arkansas, Florida, Georgia, Mississippi, Louisiana and South Carolina; the Midwest includes: Iowa, Kansas, Minnesota, Missouri, Nebraska and Wisconsin; the Southwest includes: Arizona, New Mexico, Oklahoma and Texas; and of course, California and Alaska are just those states.

Location	Points	Dogs	Bitches	Location	Points	Dogs	Bitches
Northeast	1	2	2	Southwest	1	2	3
	2	6	8		2	8	12
	3	11	14		3	15	21
	4	14	18		4	19	27
	5	19	24		5	27	39
Southeast	1	2	2	California	1	2	3
	2	6	7		2	7	9
	3	11	13		3	12	16
	4	15	18		4	16	24
	5	23	27		5	23	40
Midwest	1	2	2	Alaska	1	2	2
	2	6	7		2	3	4
	3	11	13		3	4	6
	4	16	18		4	5	7
	5	25	27		5	6	10

The points refer to the number of points earned if a given number of dogs or bitches are showing. For example, if you had a dog or a bitch winning at a show held in Maine, and eleven dogs or fourteen bitches (including yours) showed that day, your dog or bitch would earn three points toward its championship (a major). If you were showing in Alaska, eleven dogs or bitches would give you more than you needed for a five point major! In Alaska you would earn a three point major with only four dogs or five bitches (including yours). In Wisconsin, if twelve dogs showed, your dog would have earned a major, but if you were showing a bitch and twelve bitches showed, you would only earn two points, which is NOT a major, because fourteen bitches are needed to earn three points in Wisconsin, even though it only requires twelve dogs.

The area of the country where the show is held is the deciding factor, not the home of the dog. Thus, a dog owner traveling from one area of the country to another will need to keep in mind the different point scales when computing their points.

No matter how many entries are attending a show, five points is the most that will be earned. Even if the show is a large "Specialty" (a show which has been recognized by a regional or national Dalmatian Club and attracts hundreds and hundreds of entries) it will still only award five points, but as you can see from our Hall of Fame, winning at a Specialty Show will be considered more prestigious simply because of the larger number of entries. Breeders often mention "Specialty" wins because of the enhanced prestige.

Breeds with fewer dogs, or breeds with fewer dogs showing, will have very different numbers. Pulik, a relatively unknown breed, showing at the same show might need only two dogs or bitches for a point, three dogs or bitches for two points, four dogs or bitches for three points, and six dogs or bitches for five points! This is because there are far fewer Pulik whelped and shown than there are Dalmatians. If the breed becomes popular and more dogs are shown in one area of the country, the number of dogs needed for points will begin to go up each year. When the number of entries in a breed falls, the number of dogs needed for points will go down the following year. In this way, AKC limits the number of champions in each breed or variety to about 150 to 200 per year. A listing of points in the area can be found in the show catalog for each breed entered at the show, or you can call AKC Event Records Department for a copy of the point system. The new point system is printed each year in April and goes out with the AKC Calendar of Events, a monthly publication listing shows across the country for the next several months.

As you may have noticed, in the world of dog shows, a "dog" is a male — and only a male — and a female is a "bitch." Classes in dog shows are divided by dogs and bitches. The top winning dog will be "Winners Dog," and the top winning female will be named "Winners Bitch." The best between them is the "Best of Winners."

In conformation competition, all entries for the class enter the ring at the same time. The judge looks at the entire class, standing, from the side and moving around the ring at the trot. The judge then "goes over" each entry, that is to say, he looks at the teeth and puts his hands on each dog to feel the structure. Each entry is then moved at the trot and the judge looks at the movement as the dog goes away, from the side, and as the dog returns to the judge. While in the ring, dogs

(Continued on page 97)

HALL OF FAME

THE FOLLOWING SECTION IS A SHOWCASE FOR STARS OF THE BREED. All of the dogs pictured on the following pages are title holders. These animals will give you an idea how current outstanding individuals of the breed look and what bloodlines produce these qualities. The breeders and kennels listed on these pages represent a range of style within the breed. They have also been selected from across the country, giving you a chance to talk to a breeder in your area.

We congratulate the breeders and owners of these dogs for their dedication to fine Dalmatians. Their time and effort insure the success of their dogs, and the continuation of the breed.

Here is an explanation of some of the titles you will see:

Ch. - champion — conformation titles precede the name. A listing of abbreviations of countries indicates that the dog is a champion of record in each of the countries outside the United States as listed. If no country is indicated, the dog is an AKC (American Kennel Club) champion. The designation BISS (Best in Show Specialty) and BIS (Best in Show) are sometimes listed before a Ch. title. Although these are not formal titles they signify prestigious conformation victories.

WORKING TITLES

United Kennel Club working titles also precede the name. Most working titles will follow the name of the dog, as will titles of breed club recognition.

CD - Companion Dog, an obedience title.
CDX - Companion Dog Excellent, the next level of obedience.
UD - Utility Dog, the highest level of obedience title. Abbreviations of countries before an obedience title indicates that the dog holds obedience titles in each of the countries listed.
RD - Road Trial title
RDX - Road Trial Excellent, the next level of Road Trial.
TT - Temperament Tested.
CGC - Canine Good Citizen, a title awarded by AKC through a specific test of obedience and temperament.
ROM - breed club designation indicating a dog which has produced the required number of titled puppies.

Please note that minor discrepancies in the presentation of titles are the result of breeder preference and lack of a universal protocol.

HALL OF FAME ✧ 65

FRONT COVER DOG:

"Ko Ko" belonged to Dr. and Mrs. Chris Fetner and was the first liver and white champion for Coachman Kennel. She was bred by the kennel's founders, Bill and Jean Fetner, and handled to her championship by their daughter-in-law, Phyllis. Ko Ko's littermates were Ch. Coachman's Red Carpet, Ch. Coachman's Chocolate Soldier, and Coachman's Cherri Jubilee (13 points - both majors). All four liver puppies went on to contribute to the breed as show dogs and breeding stock whose get are in the pedigrees of many top kennels of today. Coachman breeds both liver and white and black and white Dalmatians. Originally blacks were preferred, but today livers are a big part of our breeding program.

```
                                                              Eng. Ch. Colonsay April Jest
                                       Ch. Colonsay Olaf the Red
                                                              Elizabeth of Mermaid
                       Ch. Blackpool Copper Courier
                                                              Ch. Willowmount Fudge Fascinator
                                       Blackpool Copper Caboose
                                                              Ch. Madamoiselle Koko
Ch. Coachman's Cup O' Tea (1973-1983)
                                                              Ch. Dottidale Jo Jo
                                       Ch. Dalhalla Thunderbolt
                                                              Chloe's Jane of East Norwich
                       Coachman's Coffee Break
                                                              Ch. Lord Jim
                                       Ch. Coachman's Carte Blanche
                                                              Ch. Coachman's Three Cheers
```

Coachman Kennels, Reg.

DALMATIANS   EXCLUSIVELY

Jean & Wm. W. Fetner   Chris & Phyllis Fetner
9195 W. Graham Rd   4640 Melissa Ln
Rocheport, MO 65279   Dallas, TX 75229
(573) 874-2360   (214) 373-7206

"MAN'S AND HORSE'S BEST FRIENDS"

REAR COVER DOG:

```
                                                              Int'l Ch. Elmcroft Coacher
                                       Kingcrest Mischief Maker
                                                              Lady Mischief of Coachroad
                       Kingcrest Pony Boy
                                                              Ch. Cressbrook Bang
                                       Am Ch. Kingcrest Constellation
                                                              Taffeta of Tattoo
Ch. Coachman's Cakewalk (1951 - 1963)
                                                              Chan-Dal-Sad Bandit
                                       Am Ch. Chan-Dal-Sad Snafu
                                                              Four-in-Hand Sweethart
                       Am Ch. Fobette's Frishka, CD
                                                              King Cal of Zane
                                       Ch. Prancing Lady of Fobette
                                                              Duchess of Zane
```

Pictured is our first homebred champion. **Ch. Coachman's Cakewalk.** This great bitch finished before one year with four majors and a Non-Sporting Group! She was in our first litter, whelped July 8, 1951 ~ We are very proud to say that from that time on, Coachman has played a major part in the founding of such prominent kennels as: Tuckaway ~ Altamar ~ Erin ~ Cannal-Side ~ Royal Coach ~ Ye Dal ~ Diamond-Dee ~ Gallopade. Numerous others have linebred on Coachman dogs to produce their winners. We are still active today with judging the breed and family breeding.

CH. RS 'LIL' MISS MEGADOTS' TNG

                        Ch. Merry-Go-Round Bentley
             Am/Can Ch. Merry-Go-Round XKE
                      Lucille of Schultz Acres
      Ch. Riverside's Soloflex CCR MGR
                      Ch. Merry-Go-Round Bentley
             Ch. CCR's Lady Sarah of MGR
                      Fantasy's Freckled Miss, CD
Ch. RS 'Lil' Miss Megadots' TNG
                      Ch. Merry-Go-Round Bentley
             Am/Can Ch. Merry-Go-Round XKE
                      Lucille of Schultz Acres
      Ch. Mika's Cindy Loo Hoo
                      Okie's Cash Domino
             Mike's Little Miss Domino
                      Little Miss Marker

Pictured at two years of age, Dotty finished her championship rapidly with five majors and a Best of Breed over Specials. She is an actively campaigned Dalmatian in multi-Breed/Group exhibition. Her outstanding Dalmatian type is superceded only by her unparalleled coaching movement. She has a lovely temperament and the personality of a "tom-boy," as might be expected from her unique freckled face. At TNG Dalmatians, our breeding program focuses on the improvement of the Dalmatian type, temperament and movement. Litters are planned years in advance and reared with the utmost attention to proper neurological stimulation, socialization and physical development. Puppies are available only to carefully qualified prospective homes.

Irvin B. Krukenkamp, M.D.  The Next Generation Dalmatians
20 Fenton St. (508) 877-8334
Framingham, MA 01701

CH. CHALKHILLS FELONY

```
                                  Ch. Judici de Montjuic
                  Ch. Sabre De Montjuic
                                  Ch. Farga De Montjuic
          Chalkhills Dale Earnhardt
                                  Ch. Buffrey Jobee
                  Ch. Cheerio Top O' The Morning
                                  Ch. Cheerio Simply Smashing
  Ch. Chalkhills Felony
                                  Ch. Judici de Montjuic
                  Ch. Saig De Montjuic
                                  Ch. Farga De Montjuic
          Ch. Holque De Montjuic
                                  Ch. Knightstone Huntsman
                  Petjada De Montjuic
                                  Ch. Cheerios Covadonga
```

Chalkhills Dalmatians has been breeding fine Dalmatians for thirty-five years. These "Dals with Distinction" include several champion studs which stand at service, show and pet puppies and occasionally adult dogs for good homes.

Patricia Wallace-Jones & J.R. Jones
200 N. Olinda Dr.
Brea, CA 92621

Chalkhills Dalmatians
(714) 996-6099

AM/CAN CH. DELUXE HIGH FASHION DOTS, CGC

                  Ch. Lord Jim
           Ch. Count Miguel of Tuckaway
                  Ch. Tuckaway Dinah
    Am/Can Ch. Saratoga's Missouri Outlaw
                  Ch. Crestview Dan Patch
           Ch. Saratoga's Crestview Dolly
                  Ch. Saratoga of Santana C
Am/Can Ch. Deluxe High Fashion Dots, CGC
                  Am/Can Ch. Paisley's Peterbilt Am/Can CDX, TT
           Ch. Markmaker Elijahari O Paisley, CDX
                  Ch. Paisley's Quinda-Brit, CD
    Ch. Lady Mattie Lovely Dots
                  Dahar's Horseplay
           Molly Keegon of Kansas City
                  Sugar Creek Holly

"Gucci" is the foundation dog of Deluxe Dalmatians of Kansas City. A multiple Best of Breed winning and Group placing dog in both the United States and Canada, Gucci is a solid dog with excellent movement and outstanding temperament. Currently, his son, Deluxe Dynamite Extrordinair, "Ike," is following in his dad's "paw steps" and is half-way to his titles in the U.S. and Canada with Best of Breeds in both countries. Although we breed on a very limited basis, we are always happy to talk with anyone interested in sharing their life with a Dalmatian.

Julie & Ron Lux
428 East 74th Terrace
Kansas City, MO 64131

Deluxe Dalmatians
(816) 926-0435
FAX (816) 926-0713

AM/CAN CH. PROCTOR'S DAPPLED HI-FLYER "MAVERICK"

```
                                        Ch. Bob Dylan Thomas of Watseka, CD
                        Am/Bra/Int Ch. Annle N. Belrins Dylan Flyer
                                        Ch. Annle's High Hopes
            Ch. Esquires Razzamatazz
                                        Ch. Long Last Living Legend
                        Ch. Long Last Liberated Lady
                                        Greenway's Tap Dancer
Am/Can Ch. Proctor's Dappled High Flyer
                                        Ch. Count Miguel of Tuckaway
                        Ch. Proctor's Hi-Ho Cheerio, CD
                                        Ch. Washakie Belleamie (Eng. Impt.)
            Proctor Onyx Jewel of the Mt.
                                        Ch. Beauregard O'Hara of Proctor
                        Ch. Proctor's Pennies From Heaven
                                        Ch. Paisley of Proctor, CD
```

Am/Can Ch. Proctor's Dappled Hi-Flyer, was the Number one Dalmatian in the USA for 1991, 1992, and 1993 (Pedigree Breed System). Maverick defeated more Dalmatians in a year during 1992, and again in 1993, than any other Dalmatian in the history of the Breed. He is currently the Number 3 Dalmatian of all times! Proctor Dalmatians has been exhibiting Dalmatians in conformation and obedience since 1968. Our Dalmatians are bred first for sound temperaments, then as healthy fun-loving house pets, and finally as very successful show dogs. We have over 80 Champions and many obedience and tracking title holders. All our dogs are BAER hearing tested and all breeding stock is OFA. We are members of the Dalmatian Club of America, Dalmatian Club of Northern California, and Dalmatian Club of Canada.

Kenneth E. & Eva E. Berg
136 Longfield Place
Moraga, CA 94556

Proctor Dalmatians
(510) 376-0136
FAX (510) 376-9032

CH. OAKDAL SHAZAM

```
                                              Ch. Tuckaway Call Me Clancy
                         Ch. Tuckaway Rex Chapman Blue
                                              Ch. Tuckaway Time
          Ch. Tuckaway Le'Baron
                                              Ch. Tuckaway Sunny's Halo
                         Ch. Tuckaway Lady's Secret
                                              Lady Coachman
Ch. Oakdal Shazam
                                              Ch. Count Miguel of Tuckaway
                         Ch. Alfredrich Handsome Tall'N Dark
                                              Ch. Sunkist Singalong
          Folklore Oakdal DD Firesprte
                                              Ch. Indalane's Rhett Butler
                         Ch. Firesprite's Trixi Dixi, CD
                                              Ch. Firesprite Trix O'Star Seeker
```

"Drew" is definitely making his mark in the Dalmatian ring. He completed his championship by winning Best of Breed and Group I at just seventeen months of age. Drew has get from three different litters that are pointed — all from the puppy classes. One daughter acquired two Group placements before she was eight months old! Drew's flowing movement, correct size, lovely markings and joyful attitude have made him popular with breeders and judges alike.

Suzanne Stoll
54400 E. 130th Rd.
Miami, OK 74354

Oakdal Dalmatians
(918) 542-1400

CAN CH. IMPERIAL STORM FRONT

```
                                    Ch. Fireman's Freckled Friend
                    Ch. Tuckaway Augusta
                                    Ch. Bottoms Up Sentmentl Journey
    Am/Can Ch. Tuckaway St. Andrews
                                    Ch. Tuckaway Sunny's Halo
                    Ch. Tuckaway Havanip
                                    Ch. Tuckaway Secondhand Rose
Can Ch. Imperial Storm Front
                                    Ch. Little Slam's Deja Vu II
                    Ch. Little Slam's Lucky Play, Am/Can CD
                                    Ch. Little Slam's Lucky Charm
    Imperial Queen's Gambit
                                    Jaybar's Brody To The Max
                    Jaybar's Calico Mine
                                    Bremans Highsierra Marble
```

Imperial Dalmatians was established with the intention of producing sound Dalmatians with excellent temperaments. "Stormy" is an exciting young example of what to expect from an Imperial Dalmatian. He is not only pleasing to look at, but a joy to live with. His charming personality and even-tempered disposition make him a wonderful companion as well as both a conformation and obedience animal. Imperial is dedicated to breeding the "whole" animal. All of our breeding stock is OFA certified clear of hip dysplasia and BAER tested for bilateral hearing. Stormy's entire litter was BAER bilateral, as was his mom's first litter. Stormy earned his Canadian Championship at one year of age and is also an American Specialty Winner.

Dennis & Carol Herbold
14713 Grayville Dr.
La Mirada, CA 90638

Imperial Dalmatians
(310) 944-8497

CH. CENTURION CENTERSTAGE

```
                              Ch. Pill Peddlers St. Nicholas
                Ch. Tuckaway Bottoms Up Gusto, CD
                              Lady Coachman
   Ch. Centurion Coachman
                              Ch. Coachmans Trump Card
                Ch. Coachmans Fancy Chocolates
                              Ch. Coachmans Zanzibar Clove
**Ch. Centurion Centerstage**
                              Ch. Omegas Top Premiere
                Ch. Centurion Thunder Burstin, CD
                              Ch. Centurion Cloudburst, CD
   Centurion Spencer
                              Ch. Indalane Bryan's Knockout
                Ch. Centurion Rainbow
                              Showcase Centurion Sanpiper
```

"Cleo" is an example of the superior quality in both type and temperament that Centurion has been producing during the past twenty five years. A multiple Best in Show winner, ranked fifth in the U.S. in 1994, Cleo is now an important link in our breeding program. With Elaine's background in socialization training and animal behavior and as an AKC judge, Centurion Dalmatians continues to produce quality pups for both show and family pets. In addition to producing over forty champions, Centurion has been involved in nearly every aspect of Dalmatians, including agility, obedience, tracking and has extensive knowledge of the breed.

Owner:
Elaine Ann Lindhorst
Dr. Barry Gardner

Breeder:
Elaine & Paul Lindhorst
49 Oak Springs Ct.
St. Charles, MO 63304
(314) 441-5298

CH. SMITHFORGED BRIGHT IDEA

```
                                      Ch. Omega's Top Premiere
                          Ch. Centurion Thunder Burstin, CD
                                      Ch. Centurion Cloudburst
         Am/Can Ch. Centurion Jaunty Jim
                                      Ch. Count Miguel of Tuckaway
                          Soldal Centurion Sassafras
                                      Centurion Limited Edition
Ch. Smithforged Bright Idea
                                      Ch. Lord Jim
                          Ch. Count Miguel of Tuckaway
                                      Ch. Tuckaway Dinah
         Ch. Firewag'ns Bobby Sue
                                      Ch. Jimmy Crack Corn of Croatia
                          Ch. Firewag'ns Lucinda of Croatia
                                      Ch. Melody Joleen of Croatia
```

"Josh" exemplifies our strict ethical guideline to produce Dalmatians of sound MIND and BODY! He is an excellent sire, producing his wonderful temperament, strong topline, gorgeous front and rear, correct size and strong true movement. We pride ourselves in using every tool available in evaluating our litters, so that each puppy is perfectly matched to their new home. We were pioneers for the BAER Hearing test and are now involved with education for the Puppy Temperament Test (PTT). Our pedigrees contain the top bloodlines in the U.S. and Canada to insure our sound MIND and BODY policy.

Gary L. & Joan M. Smith
1610 Black Road
Joliet, IL 60435-3860

Smithforged Dalmatians
(815) 744-3981

AM/CAN CH. LDY DAPS STRSNSTRYPS OF D.C.'S, AM/CAN CD, CGC

```
                                    Am/Braz Ch. Annle N Belrins Dylan Flyer
                   Ch. Esquired Razzamatazz
                                    Ch. Long Last Liberated Lady
     Ch. Proctor's Dappled High-Flyer
                                    Ch. Proctor's Hi-Ho Cheerio, CD
                   Proctor's Onxy Jewel of the Mt.
                                    Ch. Proctor's Pennies From Heaven
Am/Can Ch. Ldy Daps Strsnstryps of D.C.'s, Am/Can CD, CGC
                                    Ch. Lo-Mars Sundance Kid
                   Ch. Pic-A-Dilly's Tyler Z Ber-nel
                                    Ch. Pic-Dilly's Miss Bonnie Blue
     Patz N' NY's Lady Annastashia
                                    Ch. Karastella Choo Choo Of MGR
                   Ch. Patz Prim & Proper, CD
                                    Ch. MGR N' Patz Coffee Tea Or Me
```

Although Ravin Dalmatians is a relatively young kennel located in Billings, Montana, we have experienced consistent success with our dogs. We have been raising Dalmatians for fewer than ten years, so we rely on top kennels across the country when selecting our dogs. We not only breed, but also compete in conformation shows internationally and have had great success in the obedience rings. The goal of Ravin Dalmatians is to raise, show and compete with Dals that not only meet the standard, but are healthy, have supreme temperament, and become lifelong friends to their human companions.

Patrick D. & Linda A. Jones
353 Rolling Hills Rd.
Billings, MT 59105

Ravin Dalmatians
(406) 256-0107

CH. DAPPER-DAN'S PONGO, UD
(Feb 5, 1983 - Feb 27, 1996)

```
                                      Ch. Coachman's Canicula
                        Ch. Tuckaway Gallant Man
                                      Ch. Labyrinth Sleigh Belle
          Ch. Tuckaway the Preakness
                                      Ch. Coachman's Canicula
                        Rose Hill's Domine
                                      Ch. Crown Jewel's Sparklin' Gold
Ch. Dapper-Dan's Pongo, UD
                                      Ch. Valto's Taurus
                        Ch. Spotted Dapper-Dan, UDT, Can CDX
                                      Abigail Charisma
          Dapper-Dan's Katy Lane
                                      Ch. Ramatan's Ezekiel
                        Ramatan's Country Sunshine
                                      Ramatan's Jubilee Joy
```

After finishing his Championship, Pongo was owner-handled as a Special. He also excelled in the obedience ring, ranking in the top ten Dalmatians nationally in Open and Utility competition. He won Veteran Champion twice at regional Specialties and won the Veteran's Obedience class at the 1993 and 1994 National Specialty (at age 10 and 11). His kids continue his legacy, competing in obedience, agility, and conformation. Pongo was BAER bilateral, and all his litters are BAER and temperament tested. Pongo combined beauty and brains and was the perfect companion dog, in or out of the ring.

Bronwyn Schoelzel
194 Chestnut Hill Rd.
Litchfield, CT 06759

Dapper-Dan Dalmatians
(203) 567-8518

AM/CAN CH. BELLE AIRE'S STAR E KNIGHT, CGC, RD

                                      Aust/Eng/Int Ch. Psychic Power at Pampard
            Eng Ch. Brythennek Basil Fawlty
                    Eng Ch. Washakie Winona
Ch. Knightstone Huntsman (English import)
                    Eng Ch. Washakie Spotlight
            Washakie Tanya
                  Eng. Ch.Washakie Wishing Well
Am/Can Ch. Belle Aire's Star E Knight, CGC, RD
                  Ch. Tuckaway's The Pill Peddler
            Pill Peddler's Jack
                  Tuckaway Ruffian
Belle Aire's Bonnie Blue
                  Ch. Chocolate Chip of Quaker Acre, CD
            S and P's September Storm
                  Ch. Beaverdam's Salt and Pepper

"Joe E" exemplifies the Belle Aire Dal — sound in both body and mind! Joe E is a multiple Best In Specialty and Group winner; Top Ten two consecutive years. He is producing champions and obedience titled kids, including Best in Show and Best in Specialty Sweeps winners, plus the first Dal in the east (only the fourth in history) to obtain a UKC agility title. Joe E holds a CGC and an RD title. Belle Aire breeds Dalmatians for conformation, competition and companionship.

Tina Thomas Smith
1220 Water Plant Rd.
Zebulon, NC 27597

Belle Aire Dalmatians
(919) 269-4683

CH. FIRELINE'S INDISCREET ESQ

```
                                    Ch. Paisleys Best Bet Yet
                    Ch. Long Last' N Tailsmans Topgun
                                    Ch. Long Last Solar Flare
    Ch. Esquires MVP
                                    Ch. Long Last Black Chrome
                    Ch. Esquires Essence of Long Last
                                    Ch. Long Last No Frills
Ch. Fireline's Indiscreet Esq
                                    Ch. Forrest Ranger of Proctor, CDX
                    Ch. Forrest Fire, TT
                                    Ch. Forrest Greensleaves, CD
    Ch. Snowdot's Fireline of Proctor, CD
                                    Am/Can Ch. Joe Forrester of Proctor, CD
                    Proctor's Hopi K of Snowdot
                                    Ch. Hopi Kachina Full Circle
```

"Chief," who was my first Dalmatian, finished his championship with three majors, and a reserve at my first Dalmatian Nationals in 1990 from the 12-18 month class. This was my beginning in Dals after being a Doberman Pinscher breeder for twelve years. All my dogs are great companions and friends. My philosophies on breeding are to breed with the standard in mind, but also to have dogs with sweet temperaments, intelligence, and most of all good health. Now I have combined bloodlines from several well known kennels, and am continuing to work towards the betterment of the breed.

Mary A. Squire
P.O. Box 5063
Reno, NV 89513

Kastle Kennels
(702) 677-1036

BISS CH. MELODY TIMBER TRAIL

                        Ch. Indalane Handsome of Croatia
               Ch. Melody Mountain Music of Croatia, CD
                       Ch. Miss Camielle of Croatia
    Ch. Melody Fire On The Mountain, CD
               Am/Int'l/Mex Ch. Don Juan Tenorio De La Mancha
                  Ch. Melody Kiss Of Fire
                        Melody Angel Fire
BISS Ch. Melody Timber Trail
                        Ch. Melody Jester
               Int'l Ch. Melody Ring Of Fire of BB, CD
                       Crestview Branded Beauty
    Ch. Gem City Flash Of Fire
                     Ch. Gem City's High Roller, CD
                 Ch. Captivating Kate Of Gem City
                        Melody Mateus

Timber gets credit for my love of beautiful Dals and my philosophy "Preserving Dalmatians for Future Generations." His greatest claim to fame was winning the 1989 Dalmatian Club of Greater New York Specialty show at the tender age of fifteen months. Timber was one of the top twenty-five Dals two out of the three years he was shown, and always owner handled. I still remember my humble beginnings and welcome newcomers to call for information on this wonderful breed.

Sherryl Smith
1032 Wolfe Rd.
Abilene, TX 79602-6335

Spanner Dalmatians
(915) 698-8494

CH. HOLLYTREE'S COPPER CHELSEA, UD

                    Ch. Jabar's Jack In The Box
            Ch. Karastella Cadillac Of MGR
                    Ch. Karastella Flash Of Electra
      Ch. Merry-Go-Round Cholo O' Chelsea
                    Am/Can Ch. Dandy Dan Of Coachmaster
            Ch. MGR Merry Maker of Patz
                    Ch. Limestone's Crescendo
Ch. Hollytree's Copper Chelsea, UD
                    Ch. Lord Jim
            Ch. Tuckaway Traveler Indalane, TT
                    Ch. Tuckaway Dinah
      Touchstone's Hello Holly, UD
                    Ch. Jameson Of Shawnee
            Ch. Touchstone Sassy Sorceress, CDX, TT
                    Colonial Coach Enchantress

Beautiful, intelligent, gentle, and a loving friend, Copper is a family member. A champion, a Utility Dog, and a multiple top-ranked obedience dog for nine years running, Copper represents Hollytree Dalmatians in the Hall of Fame. Our goal is not only to breed well-balanced, correctly proportioned, healthy Dalmatians, but to also breed intelligent, sound, and easily trainable Dals for obedience, tracking, agility, and road trials. We believe Dalmatians "can do!" Our puppies are raised in the home, BAER hearing tested, and aptitude tested for each individual owner. Inquiries for loving show, obedience, and pet homes are welcome. Hollytree — enjoying, loving, raising, and training Dalmatians — since 1978. Member: Dalmatian Club of America, Huntsville Obedience Training Club, Huntsville Kennel Club.

Bob, Gilda and Alison Aguilera
402 S. Edgemont Circle
Huntsville, AL 35811

Hollytree Dalmatians
(205) 851-9484

CH. CENTENNIAL DOCTOR PEPPER

                              Ch. Lord Jim
                    Ch. Count Miguel Of Tuckaway
                              Ch. Tuckaway Dinah
          Ch. Firewag'ns Kracker Jack
                              Ch. Jimmy Crack Corn Of Croatia
                    Ch. Firewag'ns Lucinda Of Croatia
                              Ch. Melody Joleen Of Croatia
Ch. Centennial Doctor Pepper
                              Ch. He's So Handsome From Dalmatia
                    Ch. Centennial's Daniel Webster
                              Ch. Kelly Spark Of Firesprite, CD
          Centennial Extra Terrestial
                              Ch. Crestview Spark O' Firesprite
                    Firesprites Misty Morn
                              Ch. Paisley's Ebony Coachlight

In 1993, Doctor Pepper became the all-time Best of Breed winning Liver Dalmatian, retiring as a Special with 105 Best of Breed wins since earning his Championship in May of 1987. An excellent producer at stud, Doctor Pepper has an enviable record for hearing (all twelve litters sired to date have been entirely BAER tested), temperament and conformation. A number of his get are presently being shown and others, now Champions, are enjoying their lives as loving companions. As the foundation stud dog of Dals of Doctor Pepper, watch for his generations to come.

Peter Capell
1838 West Grace St.   Dals of Doctor Pepper
Chicago, IL 60613-2724   (773) 871-8735

AM/CAN CH. SNOWOOD OPTIMIST

                                      Ch. Sunnyglen's Spencer for Hire
                      Ch. Long Last Perfect for Paisley
                                      Ch. Long Last Solar Flare
        Ch. Paisleys Pointblank
                                    Ch. Classic All That Jazz
                      Ch. Paisley N Tucks Eureka
                                    Ch. Paisley N Tucks A Hitchcock, CD
Am/Can Ch. Snowood Optimist
                                    Ch. Fireman's Freckled Friend
                      Ch. Madurhason's Opening Night
                                    Madurhason's Amy Lowell
        Ch. Snowood Blackcherry Optimist
                                    Ch. Sir Ike of Croatia
                    Ch. Snowood Ja Samjedan
                                    Snowood Dancer of Paisley, CD

"Demitri" is our twenty-fifth homebred Champion. Although we had Dalmatians for many years, Snowood Dalmatians officially began in 1982 with our first "show dog." Our breeding program is conducted on a small scale. Our dogs are house dogs and a part of the family. We breed for good temperament and sound bodies, using only selected dogs of outstanding quality and disposition. In placing our puppies and older dogs, we are looking for families and individuals who have the time and willingness to deal with a Dalmatian. Dalmatians are moderate size but have an enormous amount of energy and strength. Although we love the breed, Dalmatians are not for everybody!

Meg & Mike Hennessey
PO Box 632
Elgin, IL 60121-0632

Snowood Dalmatians
(815) 597-4601
Email: Snowood @ worldnet.ATT.NET

AM/CAN CH. ALFREDRICH HANDSOME TALL 'N DARK

                                    Am/Can Ch. Coachman's Chuck-A-Luck
                  Ch. Lord Jim
                                    Coachman's Candy Cane
          Ch. Count Miguel of Tuckaway
                                  Ch. Coachman's Canicula
                  Ch. Tuckaway Dinah
                                  Ch. Labyrinth Sleigh Belle
Am/Can Ch. Alfredrich Handsome Tall 'N Dark
                                  Can Ch. Darlington's Mouki
                Am/Can Ch. Evomack's Tsar of Carlsbad
                                  Ravensglen Road Runner
            Am/Can Ch. Sunkist Singalong
                                Am/Int/Mex Ch. Melody Ring of Fire of BB, CD
                Am/Int/Mex Ch. Melody Penny Lane
                                Ch. Melody Crimson and Clover, CD

Chum is displaying the ideal blend of type, total soundness, outstanding ring presence and showmanship. His winning and producing record support the above. Chum has six BIS's and is one of the top specialty winning Dals in the history of the breed. He is a prepotent sire for his pedigree, producer of over eighty American Champions, sixty Canadian Champions who received Top Awards at specialties and Group and Best in Show winners. He is the sire of the top Best in Show female of all time, K.C, and has sired the most Dalmatian Club of America winners to date.

J. Richard Millaire and Al Kay
1794-500 West Road RR #3   Alfredrich Perm. Reg.
Casselman, ON, Canada K0A 1M0   (613) 443-3567

CH HIDEAWAY'S SCOTS OF WASHAKIE

```
                              Dalinda Dandino Dancer
                    Ch. Review At Knightstone
                              Knightstone Tzigane
          Am/Eng Ch. Washakie Dancing Brave
                              Ch. Washakie Debonaire
                    Washakie Taboo
                              Int Ch. Washakie Psychedlic
Ch.  Hideaway's  Scots  Of  Washakie
                              Ch. Brythennek Basil Fawlty
                    Ch. Knightstone Huntsman
                              Washakie Tanya
          Ch. Hideaway's Agatha Christie
                              Ch. Indalane Bryans Knockout
                    Ch. Highwoods Lady Of Summerhill
                              Ch. S & P Starlet Of Summerhill, CD
```

"Boswell" is the result of very selective breeding. His Dam's littermate, American, Italian, Monaco, European and International Champion, Hideaway's Summerhill Knight was the Number One Dalmatian in Europe, 1991. His sire, American English, Ch. Washakie Dancing Brave is the Best of Breed winner at the prestigous Crufts Dog Show in England for 1995; following his sister's win there in 1994. Hideaway Dalmatians has been associated with breeding and exhibiting Dalmatians since 1979 and is always available for questions and will gladly refer prospective owners to breeders nearest their home.

Billy & Mollie Jackson
1165 Lazy Boy Lane
Winston-Salem, NC 27103

Hideaway Dalmatians
(910) 765-1591

COACHMAN'S CITY STYLE

```
                              Ch. Count Miguel Of Tuckaway
                      Ch. Fireman's Freckled Friend
                              Diamond D's Dot To Dot
              Ch. Tuckaway Augusta
                                      Am/Can Ch. Tuckaway Bottoms Up Gusto, CD
                      Ch. Bottoms Up Sentmentl Journey
                                      Ch. Bottoms Up Somebody Special
     Coachman's City Style
                                      Ch. Coachman's Coat Of Arms, CD
                      Ch. Coachman's Trump Card
                                      Ch. Coachman's Loving Cup, CD
              Coachman's City Lights
                                      Am/Eng Ch. Buffrey Jobee
                      Gallopade's Royal Review
                                      Am/Can Ch. Coachman's Carte Rouge
```

Coachman Kennel was founded by Bill and Jean Fetner in 1944. Thru the combined efforts of Chris and Phyllis Fetner, the Kennel has remained active in show dogs as well as obedience and pets. Coachman Kennel breeds for the betterment of the breed and because of their love for the Dalmatian. Being a very people-oriented dog, the Dalmatian needs to live in the house with people. They are trustworthy and good with children over the age of five. It is very important to the Kennel that Coachman Dalmatians have a great temperament whether it is a dog for show, obedience, or your loving pet. See two more fine Coachman dogs on the outside covers.

Chris & Phyllis Fetner
4640 Melissa Ln.
Dallas, TX 75229

Coachman Kennel
Livers & Blacks
(214) 373-7206

CH. DRIFTWOOD RAMBLER SHE'S A TEN, CDX

         Ch. Lord Jim
      Ch. Count Miguel Of Tuckaway
         Ch. Tuckaway Dinah
    Ch. Fireman's Freckled Friend
         Am/Can Ch. Kale's Chequered Coachman
      Diamond D's Dot To Dot
         Diamond D's Liberty Belle
Ch. Driftwood Rambler She's A Ten, CDX
         Ch. Long Last Living Legend
      Ch. Paisleys A Change Of Pace, CD
         Ch. Paisleys A Touch Of Class, CD
    Ch. Rambler Quintessence, CD
         Lakeside's Bit-A-Mischief
      Ch. Royal Oaks Liberty Belle
         Greenbriar's Hint Of Havoc, CD

"Button" exemplifies the versatile Dalmatian that both Driftwood and Rambler aspire to breed and own. A very successful conformation dog, Button is a specialty winner with multiple group placements. She easily earned her CD and CDX obedience titles, and she is a High in Trial winner. Button will soon begin competing in her latest endeavor, Agility, which she loves. Her children follow in her pawprints; son Can Ch. Driftwood Canadian Rambler, Am/Can CD, is well on his way to his American championship and is doing advanced obedience in both countries. Daughter Driftwood One Hot Chili entered Advanced Beginners Agility training at four months, and she won a major Best of Breed from the 6-9 month puppy class.

Breeders:
Rambler Dalmatians
Joanne & Jim Nash
1907 Alford Ave
Los Altos, CA 94024
(415) 964-0181 / FAX (415) 969-1026

Owner:
Driftwood Farm Dalmatians
Kathryn Blink
751 Laurel Ave., #327
San Carlos, CA 94070
(415) 364-9333

CH. RAZZOU OF ROBINWOOD

```
                                    Ch. Robinwood's Thief Of Hearts
                        Robinwood's Christmas Spirit
                                    Ch. Fama De Montjuic
            Ch. Cajun Bon Temps
                                    Ch. Robinwood's Ivanhoe
                        Cross-Stitch's Madeline
                                    Touchstone's Bell Star, CDX, TD
Ch. Razzou Of Robinwood
                                    Ch. Count Miguel Of Tuckaway
                        Ch. Fireman's Freckled Friend
                                    Diamond D's Dot To Dot
            Ch. Robinwood's Whispering Hope
                                    Am/Can Ch. Robinwood's Union Jack
                        Ch. Robinwood's Calico O' Kelkrist
                                    Am/Can Ch. Robinwood's Calico Of Sunwood
```

Razzou of Robinwood excels in temperament and breed type. Razzou represents Robinwood Kennel breeders John and Sara Ledgerwood's latest efforts. Champions number over thirty-five and span twenty-two years of careful breeding. Robinwood Dals are BAER tested and are mostly owner-handled. They've achieved BISS wins, numerous Group I wins, top ten national ratings, and many breed wins. Available for stud includes outstanding winners such as Ch. Robinwood's Snow Prince, Ch. Robinwood's Thief of Hearts, Ch. Robinwood's American Classic, and future star, Rodeo Star O' Albelarm-Robinwood.

John and Sara Ledgerwood
22396 Autumn Wood
Porter, TX 77365

Robinwood Dalmatians
(713) 354-3536

AM/EST/FIN CH. CHEERIO VICTORY

```
                                        Branscombes Willy Wonka
                             Ch. Labyrinth Oscar Madison
                                        Labyrinth Queen Of The Nile
                Am/Rsa/Zim Ch. Labyrinth Liberator
                                        Am/Eng Ch. Buffrey Jobee
                             Labyrinth Cuba Libre
                                        Ch. Labyrinth Lalapalooza
Am/Est/Fin Ch.  Cheerio  Victory
                                        Ch. Lord Jim
                             Ch. Count Miguel Of Tuckaway
                                        Ch. Tuckaway Diana
                Ch. Cheerio Simply Smashing
                                        Am/Eng Ch. Buffrey Jobee
                             Ch. Washakie Belle Amie
                                        Aus Ch. Washakie Marbella
```

Personality plus, fun loving, best describes our "Rio!" His champion and winning get have received this same wonderful temperament. 1994 was a banner year for Rio, earning his Estonian and Finnish Championship titles. Through June 1995, Rio was ranked number fifteen with the AKC AWA listing. Pictured as Best of Breed in '95 at the Southern New England Dal Club Specialty under judge Mrs. Allan Robson - Rio combined his winning ways with sons Guardian Taradams Van Damme (Winner's dog Southern New England Dal Club Specialty '95), and Ch. TNG's Captain Picard "Gus" (Winners Dog at the Greater Washington Dal Club Specialty '95) to win first prize stud dog. His daughter, Guardian Grace and Glory has nine points as of this writing, and she has a son with a major win at just six months of age. Gus was also BOB at GWDC Specialty '96 and has many Best of Breed and Group wins. Rio and his get are special! '96 will prove Rio to be a Breed great! Inquiries welcomed.

Dennis & Karen Trout
11821 Taneytown Pike
Taneytown, MD 21787

Guardian Ltd.
(301) 447-6418

INT'L CH. JAYBAR'S TRADEMARK

```
                                    Am/Can Ch. Merry-Go-Round XKE
                          Ch. Merry-Go-Round Mardi Gras
                                    Tanglefoot's Bonnie Blue
               MGR N Jaybar Deja Vu
                                    Ch. Karastella Cadillac Of MGR
                          Smokescreen Bonnie Of MGR
                                    Spicey Pepper Of Lacey
     Int'l Ch. Jaybar's Trademark
                                    Ch. North Star's The Sorcerer, TT
                          Am/Mex Ch. North Star's Dragonrider
                                    North Star's Devils Brew, CD, TT,
               Jaybar's Poke E Dot
                                    Sultan Pepper
                          Ch. Jaybar's Dot To Dot
                                    Jaybar's Jolee
```

"Trader" has a gentle, sweet nature that makes friends for the breed wherever he goes. He is a champion producer whose offspring share his beautiful dark eyes and excellent movement. Trader is offered at stud and his pups are available to pet and show homes. Jaybar was established in 1964 and has bred many of the Champion sires that are in the pedigrees of today's winners including Ch. Dandy Dan of Coachmaster, the sire of twenty one champions, Ch. Jaybar's Jack In The Box, who sired Ch. Karastella Cadillac of MGR, one of the top producers in the history of the breed and Am/Can/Mex Ch. Jaybar's Black Label, a multi-group winner and the first Dalmatian to be owner-handled to his championship in three countries. We continue to strive for top quality Dals that exhibit lovely temperaments which are so important in the family pet as well as in our show dogs. Trader is BAER bilateral hearing and OFA Good.

Barbara Niemeyer
9960 Bordeaux Ave.
Arleta, CA 91331

Jaybar Dalmatians
(818) 899-3439

CH. FOLKLORE 'N' FIRESPRITE WM TELL

```
                                Ch. Lord Jim
                    Ch. Count Miguel Of Tuckaway
                                Ch. Tuckaway Dinah
        Am/Can Ch. Saratoga's Missouri Outlaw
                                Ch. Crestview Dan Patch
                    Ch. Saratoga's Crestview Dolly
                                Ch. Saratoga Of Santana, CD
Ch. Folklore 'N' Firesprite Wm Tell
                                Ch. Tuckaway Traveler Indalane, TT
                    Ch. Indalane's Rhett Butler
                                Ch. Rebecca Of Indalane
        Ch. Firesprite's Trixi Dixi, CD
                                Ch. Crestview Spark O' Firesprite
                    Ch. Firesprite Trix O' Star Seeker
                                Royal Oaks Fireworks Of Lamia
```

Tell's a Bred By Exhibitor dog who's compiling an impressive list of accomplishments. A multiple Best of Breed winner with group placements, that thrilled us with back-to-back Best in Show wins! Nationally ranked in 1987 Top Ten Routledge plus top twenty-five DCA, exclusively Breeder/Owner/Handled! Sire of DCGI, Winner's Dog and Best in Sweeps. A classic Dal-passing on his charisma.

Robert & Diana Skibinski
Folklore Dalmatians
36200 State Route 303
Grafton, OH 44044   Co-owner: Norma Baley
(216) 926-3431   Firesprite Dalmatians

CH. FIRESPRITE FOLKLORE FUNSTER

          Ch. Firesprite Folklore Chip'ndale
        Ch. Firesprite's Razzel Dazzel
          Ch. Firesprite's Red Hot Mama
    Ch. Folklore's Louis L'Amour
          Ch. Folklore 'N' Firesprite Wm Tell
        Ch. Folklore Fancy Me Firesprite
          Ch. Firesprite's Glow Of Clockgate
Ch. Firesprite Folklore Funster
          Ch. Bell Ringer's Sundance
        Am/Can Ch. Firesprite N Coachlyt Gigilo
          Ch. Paisley's Ebony Coachlight
    Folk's Firesprite Cinderella
          Ch. Bob Dylan Thomas of Watseka, CD
        Ch. Classic Hello Dolly
          Ch. Melody Kiss Me Kate

Trish has already made us and her ancestors proud, winning Best of Winners at her first all breed show. Her steady effortless movement, over-all balance and fun personality have been appreciated by other breeders and judges alike. With a pedigree any girl would be proud of, she has alot to live up to, and we feel she will. She finished her championship at fifteen months of age.

Ray & Norma C. Baley
5 N 030 Ridge Lane
Bartlett, IL 60103-9608

Firesprite
(630) 289-7992

CH. FIRESPRITE'S RAZZEL DAZZEL

```
                                    Am/Can Ch. Saratoga's Missouri Outlaw
                    Ch. Folklore 'N' Firesprite Wm Tell
                                    Ch. Firesprite's Trixi Dixi, CD
      Ch. Firesprite Folklore Chip 'ndale
                                    Am/Can Ch. Firesprite N Coachlyt Gigilo
                    Firesprite's Tarbo
                                    Stripe's Firesprite's Gypsy
Ch. Firesprite's Razzel Dazzel
                                    Ch. Bell Ringer's Sundance
                    Am/Can Ch. Firesprite N Coachlyt Gigilio
                                    Ch. Paisley's Ebony Coachlight
      Ch. Firesprite's Red Hot Mama
                                    Honeylane's Mount Fuji, CD
                    Lady Cambridge III
                                    Blackeyed Susy of Bonnybrook
```

Razz finished his championship so quickly it made our heads spin. He completed his championship in a matter of months with very limited showing, winning two 3-point majors and three 4-point majors including a Best of Breed over top specials along the way. Razz has sired over 100 pups - no deaf and most litters all bilateral hearing. All this and he's a delight to live with too!

Norma C. Baley and Christine Nowacki
5 N 030 Ridge Lane
Bartlett, IL 60103-9608

Firesprite
(630) 289-7992

CH. KORCULA MIDNIGHT AMANDA, CD

                          Ch. Count Miguel Of Tuckaway
                Ch. Fireman's Freckled Friend
                          Diamond D's Dot To Dot
    Ch. Korcula Midnight Star Bret D
                          Germini's Proud Discovery
                Ch. Korcula Midnight Serenade
                          Ch. Korcula Midnight Hannah
Ch. Korcula Midnight Amanda, CD
                          Ch. Indalane's Rhett Butler
                Ch. Pic-A-Dilly's Mr. Brent Of Tara
                          Ch. Indalane's Scarlet O' Hara
    Ch. Korcula Midnight Mistress
                          Gemini's Proud Discovery
                Ch. Korcula Midnight Serenade
                          Ch. Korcula Midnight Hannah

Mandy has a beautiful temperament, always loving and playful, loves grandchildren, adults and other animals. She has been proclaimed by the mayor of Kansas City, Kansas as the official mascot of the Heartland Fire Society and Museum. This museum specializes in preserving the history of fire-fighting in the midwest. Mandy truly shines in the showring. Her grandsire was listed as #1 sire, her sire #2; and her dam #1 in 1991. As a result, Mandy and five of her littermates (out of nine) completed a championship — only the second litter in Dal history to accomplish this. For a Dalmatian with the all-around qualities of conformation, personality, and heritage, we feel Mandy ranks among the best. OFA Certified. Mandy's daughter is now a champion and two grand daughters are well on their way to their championships.

Jack and Dianna Teeter
1521 South 49th St.
Kansas City, KS 66106

DALANNA DALMATIANS

(913) 287-1609

HALL OF FAME ✧ 93

BIS/CAN/FCI INT'L/MEX CH. PINZELL DE MONTJUIC

```
                                    Eng Ch. Psychic Power At Pampard
                        Eng Ch. Brythennek Basil Fawlty
                                    Eng Ch. Washakie Winona
            BIS Ch. Knightstone Huntsman
                                    Eng Ch. Washakie Spotlight
                        Washakie Tanya
                                    Eng Ch. Washakie Wishing Well
BIS/Can/FCI/Int'l/Mex  Ch.  Pinzell  De  Montjuic
                                    Ch. Lord Jim
                        Ch. Count Miguel Of Tuckaway
                                    Ch. Tuckaway Dinah
            Ch. Cheerio's Covadonga
                                    Eng/Am Ch. Buffrey Jobee
                        Aust Ch. Washakie Belleamie
                                    Aust Ch. Washakie Marbella
```

Breeding and showing quality Dalmatians based on Top Producing bloodlines from Canada, USA and Great Britain. We raise happy healthy puppies in the house and have produced Best In Show winners both in all breed and Specialty shows in Canada, the United States and the United Kingdom. The philosophy of this small select kennel is to produce Dalmatians that are sound in body and mind for family companions whether they be show dogs or couch dogs.

Ann Goldman-Hennigan
61782 Yale Rd.
RR2 C2 Flood B
Hope, BC Canada V0X 1L0

DeMontjuic Dalmatians & Beagles
Established 1967
(604) 869-5584
FAX (604) 869-5591

CH. CIMARRON MOONSHINE WHISKEY, CGC, CD,RD

        Ch. Sunnyglen's Spencer For Hire
     Am/Can Ch. Long Last Perfect For Paisley
        Ch. Long Last Solar Flare
  Ch. Hopi Kachina Kopon
        Ch. Hopi Kachina Mosairu II, CDX, TDX
     Ch. Hopi Kachina Soyoko
        Ch. Hopi Kachina Kuwantotim, CD
Ch. Cimarron Moonshine Whiskey, CGC, CD, RD
        Ch. Melody Johnny Angel, TT
   Ch. Picadilly's Pleased As Punch, TT
        Ch. Indalane's Scarlette O'Hara
  Cimarron Stardust Memories, CD, CGC
        Am/Int'l/Mex Ch. Don Juan Tenorio De La Mancha
   Melody Sugar N'Spice Of Keegan, CD
        Royal Oaks Melody Of Keegan

Generations of consistency and quality are hallmarks of Cimarron's breeding program. We focus on mental and physical soundness — our Dals are smart and healthy as well as beautiful to look at. We believe that a well-balanced dog should have a title at both ends. Pablo has outdone himself in this regard, with Championship, Companion Dog, and Road Dog titles and a Canine Good Citizenship Award. He is currently working on a Tracking Dog title and a Weigh Pulling title as well! He exemplifies the word "versatile," as a Dalmatian should. Our puppies are well socialized and temperament tested to fit in with their new families. All of the dogs we produce or use for breeding are BAER and OFA certified. We believe in quality versus quantity and only breed a litter occasionally. Older dogs are also available on occasion, as is Champion stud service to approved bitches. Show handling, training and "moral support" are also available. We are proud of our "kids" and want you to be, too!

Cimarron Dalmatians
P.O. Box 974
Erie, CO 80516

Jena Zafiratos
(303) 828-3772
Carol J. Curlee
(303) 666-8148

CH. CROWN JEWELS BRIO BREEZE

       Crown Jewel Diamond's Beget
     Crown Jewel's Forty Carat Rock
       Robert's Gabrealle Gabby
  Ch. Crown Jewel's Tiger-Eye-Mine
       Ch. Crown Jewel's Hope Diamond II
     Crown Jewel's Tani Coral
       Res Ipsa Loquitur
Ch. Crown Jewels Brio Breeze
       Ch. Woodlyn's Gamble of Watseka
     Majestic Dxtr of Coachmaster
       Coachmaster's Benedictine
  Ch. Majestic K'ls Mitzi Too
       The Grand Duke of Glory Manor
     Princess Mitzi of Edo
       Majestic Ebon Mistress

Brio, pictured here at thirteen months old, finished his championship on his first birthday, owner-handled and was 1978 Best in Futurity at DCA. He sired a champion before the age of two. We invite you to compare Brio to the Dalmatian Standard.

Dr. Billie I. Ingram
9393 Carriage Way
College Station, TX 77845

Brio Del Rey Kennels
(409) 776-8909

UCH./CH. TOUCHSTONE'S DEALER'S CHOICE, TT
DNA tested, BAER Bi-Lateral, OFA-Good

                              Ch. Jameson Of Shawnee
                  Touchstone Four On The Floor, TT
                              Colonial Coach Enchantress
    Ch. Touchstone's Wheeler Dealer, CDX, TT, CGC
                              Ch. Tuckaway Traveler Indalane, TT
                  Touchstone's Morgan LeFey, CDX, CGC, TT
                              Ch. Touchstone Sassy Sorceress, CDX, TT
UCh./Ch. Touchstone's Dealer's Choice, TT
                              Ch. Count Miguel Of Tuckaway
                  Ch. Fireman's Freckled Friend
                              Diamond D's Dot To Dot
    Eclipse Fun In The Sun
                              Ch. Tuckaway Blushing Groom
                  Bittersweet Cassandra
                              Bittersweet Summer Guest

Breeding to the standard for soundness, beauty, good health, excellent temperament, intelligence, obedience potential and trainability. Touchstone stock has resulted in over thirty champions, over sixty obedience titles, Assistance Dogs, Therapy Dogs, Tracking Dogs, CGC awards, TT's fifteen High In Trial Dalmatians, etc. Chip finished his AKC Ch. very fast with three majors, his UKC Ch. with Multiple Group wins and placings, plus Best In Show wins. Sire of Champions and major pointed get, Chip is siring top quality as expected. Puppies occasionally to qualified homes.

Sam & Cathy Murphy   Touchstone Dalmatians
8513 Knox School Rd.   (330) 894-2243
Minerva, OH 44657

are to stand at attention at all times and to behave with manners toward their handlers, the judge and other dogs.

If you have never entered a dog in a show, perhaps the best thing to do is go and see what a show is like. To attend a show, call your local kennel club, watch the newspapers, look in the phone book, which often lists yearly events in the area and will sometimes list the dog shows, call the AKC Event Records Department or call your breeder. Once you are at a show, visit the vendors around the grounds. Those selling general merchandise will usually sell calendars with the shows listed in them. Some of our vendors in the Shopping Arcade section of this book also carry these calendars.

An exhibitor gets ready to compete before the class.

Entries must be made two and a half weeks ahead of time, and a program is printed for each show, listing each dog entered, its name, owner, breeder and age. Dogs will show first. Puppy dogs, Novice dogs, Bred by Exhibitor dogs (those whose breeders are actually showing them), American Bred dogs (open to any dog bred in the United States), and Open dog. The first place winners from each class will go back into the ring to pick Winners Dog. Then the bitches show, through the same classes, and the first place winners will return for Winners Bitch. Only the top dog and bitch will win points; all other dogs and bitches will go home empty handed!

For that reason, people often hire handlers. These professionals know how to present a dog to its best advantage, and they know the judges and what certain judges are looking for in a dog. Sometimes owners will show their own dogs, and that is referred to as "owner handled." You may see that term in our Hall of Fame section. Sometimes, a dog will travel with the handler to the show and the owner does not attend at all. If your breeder sold you your dog with a contract which says he must be shown, you may be required to send the dog with a handler in order to get him "finished," that is, to earn his championship. As Dalmatians are highly competitive, it is difficult for a novice handler to win. If you are new to dog showing, it is probably wise to consider hiring a handler until you learn about dog shows and how to show your dog to his best advantage. Once you learn — there are a number of good and very successful Dalmatian owner-handlers — you may enjoy showing your own dog.

Once a dog has earned his title, he will show only in the "Best of Breed" class. Champions, and the Winners Dog and Winners Bitch for the day, will return to the ring to select the "Best of Breed." If the Best of Breed is a dog, a bitch will be chosen as "Best of Opposite Sex." If the Best of Breed is a bitch, a dog will be named Best of Opposite Sex. Only the Best of Breed will return to the group ring at the end of the day to compete in the "Group."

All breeds are divided into one of seven Groups: Sporting, Non-Sporting, Herding, Working, Terriers, Toys and Hounds. There are about fifteen to twenty breeds in each group. Dalmatians are in the Non-Sporting Group. The winner of each group will return to the Best in Show ring where the final seven dogs compete to be named the Best in the Show. You may have watched parts of the Group judging or Best in Show judging from Madison Square Garden on cable television. Other famous local shows are sometimes broadcast.

In the early days of showing, in the 1930s, all champions were in the Open Class, and "Specials Only" meant your dog was for sale or on exhibition. Almost all shows were benched, with dogs tethered with chains. There were raised platforms in the middle of the ring which the judges used to compare exhibits, and the winner was always placed "On the Block." Most of the exhibitors were people of wealth and social position, and owners seldom showed their own dogs.

Westminster was a three-day affair offering benching. Colored cards in place of ribbons were displayed on the back of each dog's bench to help the public recognize the winners. Kennel men often spent the night on the benches with the dogs.

Today, the average AKC show will have about 1,000 to 1,500 dogs entered. Some will have entries of 2,500 to 3,500. One show in Louisville, Kentucky has reached 5,000 entries! There is a lot of excitement at a show, and usually ten to twenty-five rings are being judged at once. If you do not have the judging schedule ahead of time and wish to see a certain breed, be sure to arrive as early as 8:30 in the morning. While some shows do not begin until 9:00, some shows start as early as 8:00. Each breed is judged at a certain pre-scheduled time in a specific ring. A judging schedule is available ahead of time to exhibitors and generally arrives in the mail about three to four days before the show. If you arrive too late, you may find that the breed you are interested in has already been judged early in the morning, and only the Best of Breed dog is still on the grounds. Or, the dogs may be back at their vans and cars, scattered across a large parking lot and almost impossible to find. We have very few classic Bench Shows left in this country, so dogs are not on exhibit all day. They are brought up from their cars and vans, shown, and returned to rest until their owners are ready to go home.

HOW TO KNOW A STAR

This five week old pup is already starting to learn how to "stack," or stand, for the judge.

Dog showing is a subjective sport. People who show, talk about the fine points of conformation. But almost everyone agrees that "quality" and "balance" are just as important as any single asset. Balance is reflected both in the way the front and rear of a dog go together and in the way a dog moves. It refers to the proportions of the dog, and how they all fit together. But there is another factor in a top winning dog. It is elusive, and cannot truly be defined, but it is called "presence." One breeder describes a retired show dog at eight years of age: "He came into a large room, stood there and looked at you. Everything else in the room faded away. I have never seen a photograph that does him justice. The memory of him that day is implanted in my mind forever." A show dog with presence can sometimes have a few faults. He may not be as perfect as another dog, but he has a style, a quality that, like an actor or a model, sets him apart. He is charismatic, and a judge is attracted to him.

Some dogs are called "Package Dogs." They are nice in a number of ways. They may have good parts to them, though not as good as some other entries' but they are strong in a number of different ways, and have no large faults. They are good movers and have sound conformation, balance and presence. They go together in a well-balanced package. This "package" is what makes a truly great show dog.

But remember, there is no such thing as a perfect dog, or one which wins all the time. The top winning dog at Madison Square Garden, or at the breed Nationals, may fail to get a ribbon the next day under a different judge. Opinions of judges will be different depending on their personal experiences and beliefs. The stronger the competition is between good dogs, the more disagreements there are because the finer points of judging require personal evaluation. One characteristic may be listed as a fault, but so might another on a different dog, and there is nothing to say which is better or worse. A judge may be looking at one dog with a good neck and head, but a bad tailset, while another has a wonderful topline, but a common head. These are values which must be subjectively weighed by a judge. This is a beauty contest. What a judge ultimately points at (selects as his winner) depends on his personal belief of which is a more serious fault, and what good points he values. Perhaps he will go with a dog which has no faults, but no outstanding features either. What is often taken as "crooked" judging is simply a matter of personal values on the part of the judge which may differ from those of the spectator or exhibitor. Remember, we do not ask a judge to tell us what he thinks is a perfect Dalmatian. We ask him his opinion in picking the best of what is in front of him that day. Like people, dogs may have good and bad days where they are more or less interested in showing. How well a dog *likes* to show is an important element, and gives him the "presence" he needs to be a winner.

There are no hard and fast rules determining a show dog. Any dog with full AKC registration can be a show dog by paying the entry fee, and if he has no disqualifying faults, he will be allowed to compete to the extent of completing his class. Some dogs are so average that they will consistently place under almost all judges, even in strong competition, but they will never win because although they have no faults, they have no great assets either. Others will win one day under a judge who appreciates their good qualities, and lose another day under a judge who puts emphasis on an area where they are weak. The latter have an up and down career but will probably still finish their championship before the dog with no great faults, but no great assets. Keep this in mind when you are buying a show dog, and keep it in mind when you are beginning to show.

Remember what one of our breeders says: "A good judge is one who puts up my dog, a bad judge puts up someone else's dog, and a terrible judge puts up my worst enemy's dog!" Dog showing is a competitive sport. Over the years, exhibitors learn to appreciate certain things in a dog and dislike others. Breeders develop their own style within their kennel and many believe that dogs which are not of that style are "inferior". But they are not the judge. The judge may agree with them one day and disagree with them another day. All of this is to say that if you buy a dog, one of the worst things you can do is take it to a show and ask all the other exhibitors what they think of it. The opinions you get back are more likely to reflect the feelings of the individual exhibitor toward the style, and even the breeder of the dog, than an absolute evaluation of the dog.

If you are interested in showing, enter a show and see how your dog does in competition. If he wins, enjoy your success. If he loses several shows, consider that he may not be developed enough (if he is still immature), or that you might not be able to show him to his best advantage. Sometimes a dog which cannot win as a puppy or young adult will mature into a fine show dog; he simply needed time to develop. Find a professional handler, and ask him or her about showing, or at least evaluating, your dog. These people handle a number of different breeds from a wide variety of breeders. They know, overall, what a quality dog is and what it takes to get a dog finished. Handlers are a more objective source of information than competing breeders or exhibitors.

Sometimes a judge will talk to you if you wait until after his assignment is over, though he is not required to do so and some judges do not like talking to exhibitors or novice owners. Don't expect to get all the answers at your first show, or even the first year you show. The complexity of dog showing is one of the things that interests and fascinates people in the sport, and keeps them dedicated in time and money for many years.

Good breeders will not guarantee that a puppy will be a great show dog. They will sell a pup based on his pedigree and what other, older siblings have done in the ring, and how the pup looks compared to his parents and other litters from the same bloodline. The longer a breeder has bred and shown, the better idea he or she will have on how much *potential* a pup has. But there are seldom guarantees because there are so many variables. The area of the country a dog shows in will make a difference in how fast he finishes. Who handles him and how well he is conditioned and presented will make a difference. How much the dog *enjoys* showing will make a difference. And even experiences he has in the ring during his first few months of showing will make a difference.

Novice owners frequently take a young dog to a show, and when it does not win the first time or two, they begin to drag it around to other breeders and judges and inquire about its faults. This practice is very counterproductive, because all it does is call everyone's attention to the negative parts of the dog, so that even when he does develop and would normally begin to win, everyone remembers the faults that have been pointed out early in the dog's career. Also, remember it is easier for people to make negative comments about a potential competitor than it is to recognize the good qualities and point out how to best present the strengths. That is like asking a competing coach how to improve another team! And, if you have not bought a pup from the local breeders, they may resent the fact that they were overlooked when you went outside the area. Even if you bought your dog from a local breeder, other breeders in the area may comment on the dog (either in a negative or positive way) with more of an eye on how much they like the person who sold you the dog than on how nice the dog really is. More than one dog has been sent back to a breeder because the novice owner did not feel it was "show quality," and the breeder has finished it easily.

Never expect anyone to guarantee that a puppy will be a group placing dog. Group placings are dependent on so many different things, from the competition that day to the early care a dog has received. Many people who want a group placing dog try to buy an older dog who has already started his show career and done well. Often handlers will find a dog they think has great promise and approach an owner about purchasing it. Sometimes, people who want a group placing dog will simply offer to "back" a dog which is already being shown and winning. This means that the "backer" puts his or her name on the dog and receives the fame for the dog's wins, and in return pays the bills to a greater or lesser extent, depending on the arrangement. Several Westminster Winners have been "owned" by backers who never bred or owned another dog of that breed, and who have no kennel and no intentions of ever breeding. When the dog was finished showing, he simply went back to the original owner who used him or her for breeding purposes and gave the dog a home for the rest of his life.

WORKING TITLES

Working dogs (those whose career is based on what they can do) can continue to show for many years. They get better with age, often understanding what is expected better than they did when they were young, and frequently having more patience and experience to evaluate the task. If the owner is careful to make the work fun for the dog, the dogs who compete in the working division can continue to show for many years after they retire from the conformation ring. The following are considered working titles because they judge how the dog per-

Working dogs can continue their careers for many years.

forms rather than simply what he looks like. These titles require training and natural talent. Working titles, once earned, will stay with the dog for the rest of his life, and in most cases, working titles will follow the name of the dog. You can see many of these titles on the dogs featured in the Hall of Fame. Just as dogs are bred to be conformation champions, you will see many similarities in pedigrees between dogs with working titles. A working dog must have aptitude for his job, and he must enjoy it.

OBEDIENCE

Dogs with working titles earn their titles for life through a series of performances where they earned a qualifying score, that is, a score which was high enough to earn them a "leg" on their title. Most performance competition is done on a point system, and more than one dog a day can earn points toward his title. If he performs well, he will be rewarded. Performance or working titles follow the registered name of the dog, and once earned, are printed each time the name of the dog is written.

Obedience is an event at most dog shows. Unlike conformation showing where no special training is needed to start showing a young dog, obedience dogs are required to show off-lead and through a specific set of exercises. Judging is very precise. Scoring is done by subtracting points for faults such as failing to sit square, to return fully, or to stay in step on the heel exercise. Conformation dogs do not need to sit — in fact they should *not* sit while in the ring. Obedience dogs are required to sit when the handler stops walking and when a command is given throughout the exercise program. Conformation classes and obedience classes are held at the same time, so it is very difficult, especially for a young dog and a novice handler, to adapt to the different types of showing and to work with the conflicting schedules which often develop.

Obedience dogs need to have reached a level of training so that they can go through precise movements on the command of their handlers, including heel, sit, stay and down.

An obedience dog must be by nature intelligent and willing to please. For that reason, Dalmatians are usually good competitors, especially if the handler takes care to make it fun for them.

Dogs begin with the Novice class. "A" and "B" divisions relate to the handler. "A" dogs are handled by their owners, and only one dog may be shown in the class. The "B" division allows a dog to be handled by a professional handler or trainer, and several dogs may be handled by the same owner or handler in the same class in the "B" division.

There are six exercises which score points: Heel on Leash, Stand for Examination, Heel Free, Recall, Long Sit and Long Down, with a possible total of 200. All but the Heel on Leash must be done off-lead, and a dog must score at least 50% of the available points in each exercise *and* have a total score of 170 or higher in three obedience trials (with at least six dogs in competition) to earn a CD (Companion Dog) title. Once this is earned, the dog moves up to the next level.

This level has seven exercises. Each must be precisely executed. They are: Heel Free, Drop on Recall, Retrieve on Flat, Retrieve Over High Jump, Broad Jump, Long Sit and Long Down. Three qualifying scores at three different shows are needed to earn the title of CDX (Companion Dog Excellent). Dogs may then move up to earn a UD (Utility Dog) title.

This is the highest title an obedience dog can earn. The seven exercises include scent discrimination, hand signals, and both broad and high jumps.

Almost every show has classes for obedience. They are usually held in a ring apart from the conformation showing. If you are interested in showing your dog in obedience, begin with a local obedience class. Be prepared to work with him on a daily basis for several months before you attempt to show. You may want to start showing at a local "match show." These are practice shows for both conformation and obedience. They offer no points toward a title, but they are usually small, with limited competition and no pressure, and they are a good place to begin to learn the dog show game.

Conformation and obedience are two very different kinds of activities, and they frequently attract different kinds of personalities. Even the dress is different. Obedience dog handlers wear casual clothes. Many obedience people feel that dark pants help blend with the dog and mask mistakes. Shirts and pants, even for women, are the normal attire. In conformation, especially in the East, women almost always wear dresses, suits with skirts, or skirts and blouses. Men wear sports coats and ties, except on very hot days, when the judge may indicate that the coat may be disregarded. Men are seldom seen without a tie, jeans are not appropriate, and women are almost never seen in pants. In California, and some other areas, golf shirts and pants are sometimes worn, though jeans and T-shirts are never considered appropriate.

AGILITY

Begun in 1977 in England, Agility is an obstacle course for dogs. It is fun, fast and growing in popularity each year. Dogs go through a series of obstacles, over a bridge, on teeter totters, through tunnels and barrels, between poles, and over A-frames. Dalmatians are quick and intelligent. Many of them love the ex-

In agility, the dog goes through a series of brightly colored obstacles and is scored for both time and quality of performance.

citement generated by being on the course against time, and they are good at figuring out new obstacles. Agility is an activity which is particularly well suited to the breed.

Dogs must be over six months old, and able to compete through obstacles off-lead. Dogs compete against time over the obstacles and lose points for failing to complete an obstacle as described. Qualifying scores add toward titles, but high score dogs at an event are also recognized. Call your local kennel club for details of Agility Clubs in your area; most kennel clubs have at least a few members who are interested or active in Agility and new clubs are forming every year. Agility is one of the fastest growing new sports involving dogs and attracts people from all walks of life. Several of the major dog food companies have sponsored events, and in addition to competitions, there are many Agility exhibitions at dog shows and other spectator events throughout the country each year.

For those who are very interested, there is a National Championship. A dog must qualify to compete, and for many years the finals have been held in Houston, Texas, in the

Astrodome. It has attracted dogs from all over the country and in almost all breeds. Dalmatians are usually very good at Agility. They are fast and quick thinkers with an agile body build. Each year several Dals qualify for the National Championship competition.

AKC CANINE GOOD CITIZEN TEST AND TEMPERAMENT TESTING

Recently, the AKC has added the Canine Good Citizen test. They are recognizing the need for responsible dog ownership, and the recognition of well trained pets. Most clubs put on a CGC test at least once a year. The CGC test which lasts most of a day, tests the dog's ability to do basic obedience and his attitude in meeting new people and new situations. If he passes the test, he is awarded a CGC title. Dogs are scored against a standard objective as they are with obedience and not against the other dogs in competition as they are in conformation. This means that many dogs can qualify to be awarded their CGC title on the same day. These tests are growing in popularity and more and more dogs are showing up with CGC attached to their names.

Temperament Testing is somewhat similar, though it is not done through AKC. These tests require a dog to meet friendly strangers, hostile strangers, neutral strangers, and a variety of situations. Again, the test will take up the better part of a day, but the title earned will stay with the dog for life. You will see a number of dogs in the Hall of Fame with CGC or TT at the end of their name.

A Road Trial is part obedience test and part endurance test. In this phase the dog heels to the horse. The second rider is the judge.

ROAD TRIALS

A road trial is to a Dalmatian what a field trial is to the pointer or retriever breeds or a herding trial is to the shepherd breeds. It is a test designed to gauge the Dalmatian's ability to perform the tasks it was originally bred to perform. For more than 300 years, Dalmatians have gaited beneath the coach behind the horses. Pointers point, retrievers retrieve, Dalmatians "coach."

Road trials began in the early 1900s, when dogs were tested for their ability to run beneath the coach. These early efforts apparently died out and there is not much information on them, but new rules added in the 1940s included competition for riders on horseback with no cart. Dogs "coached" by trotting at the side of the horse. After a short revival of the sport, in New England and Long Island, the trials again died out.

In 1989, a breed enthusiast named Linda Myers, of Washington, once again revived the sport and updated the rules. Since then, road trial competition has been growing in popularity at a steady pace. Ms. Myers studied the rules of the post-war road trials and the AKC obedience regulations and put together the present road trial regulations with the help of former road trial participants and present-day fanciers. In September 1989, a road trial was held in Woodinville, Washington — the first in America in forty years! Although not recognized yet by the AKC, these trials are held by permission of the Dalmatian Club of America. All participants receive a Road Trial Recognition Award certificate from the DCA. The DCA has a Road Trial Committee that is charged with updating and maintaining the

104 ✧ BASIC GUIDE TO THE DALMATIAN

Road Trial Rules and Regulations, the handbook that guides participants in the road trial procedures, and helps regional Dalmatian clubs to host these events. Rental horses are made available, and the sport has begun to be within the reach of many Dalmatian lovers.

A modern Road Trial involves several obedience tests from horseback. Dogs are judged in the hock exercise (which is similar to the heel exercise in obedience, with the dog staying at the hock of the horse), recall, stay, hock with distraction, and speed exercise. The speed exercise is interesting. Upon direction from the judge; horse, rider and dog are expected to "take off" for about thirty yards. The dog does not have to stay in the hock position, and it would not be safe if he did. Remember the handler is probably riding a rented horse, over rough unfamiliar terrain, at a gallop, with a dog. The dog is judged on whether or he can keep up with the galloping horse, and stop when the horse slows down. The Road Trial includes an endurance test of twelve and a half or twenty-five miles. Veterinarians check the dogs at different intervals, and award points at the end according to the condition of the dog. Dogs which qualify and complete twelve and a half miles earn a "Road Dog" title (RD) from the Dalmatian Club of America; those that qualify at twenty-five miles earn "Road Dog Excellent" (RDX).

There are two judges, one mounted and one on foot called the course judge. Four classes are offered. In Road Dog A classes, the dog must pass all exercises with a score of at least 51 out of a possible 100 per exercise, pass all vet checks and complete the short course of twelve and a half miles within three hours time. In this class, the rider has never competed in a road trial before and the dog has not received an RD or RDX title. In Road Dog B classes, the course is the same, but either the rider or the dogs have competed in a road trial before or the dog has an RD or RDX title. Road Dog Excellent A is the same as Road Dog A but the twenty-five mile course is run within six hours instead of the shorter distance and Road Dog Excellent B has the same qualifications as Road Dog B, but with the longer course.

Teams leave the starting point every twenty minutes. A team consists of a horse, a rider and as many as six Dalmatians. After a half-mile warm-up, the team is met by the mounted judge and the exercises are performed. The rider controls the dog(s) from his or her horse without the benefit of a leash.

Road Trials are growing steadily and new ones are added every year. So far about 90% of those who attempt them have earned qualifying scores. Dogs must be trained to follow their master on any horse under all conditions, including around cattle, other dogs, and wild game; past gunshots and through inclement weather. Dogs, horses and exhibitors must be in good enough condition to complete the endurance ride. So far, road trials have been held on bridle paths in Washington State, game farms in Pennsylvania, the blue grass of Kentucky, a cattle ranch in California, a wooded estate in South Carolina and a recreational area in Wisconsin. They are a sight to see. Breed enthusiasts and dog lovers turn out in large numbers to observe the Trials. They are unique to this unique breed

Although not commonly used for tracking, Dalmatians are very versatile and can do almost anything which is assigned to them. Tracking is a now a competitive sport, just as obedience or agility.

CARE

*D*almatians do shed. It is a fact of life. The white coat is noticeable on dark fabrics. Regular grooming will remove dead hair and keep the coat in top condition. One breeder recommends adding a tablespoon of vegetable oil to food once a day to help reduce shedding. One caution about any food additive to help skin or coat condition — it must be used every day for several weeks to make a difference.

Brushing is essential to any dog's coat. Although Dals do not require the constant coat attention of long haired breeds, a brushing once a week is beneficial. Use a brush or mitt with natural horsehair bristles (sometimes called a "hound brush) or a rubber curry to keep the coat shiny and the loose hair to a minimum. A stripping stone, which is similar to a piece of lava rock, is invaluable in ridding the coat of dead hair and flaky skin. One or two breeders recommended using a vacuum. If you begin to use the vacuum when the pup is young he will get used to the noise and suction of the upholstery attachment. Many dogs actually enjoy the feeling as a massage.

During the winter your Dal may exhibit flaky dandruff, usually due to the lack of humidity in the home. A solution of half Alpha Keri oil to half water, sprayed and worked into the coat with a brush will help. To get rid of the flaking quickly on a cosmetic level, put mouthwash in a spray bottle and lightly mist the dog. This treatment dissolves the skin cells, and leaves the dog smelling "minty fresh!"

Also, during the winter a Dal's ears may become dry around the edges and "crack." or even bleed. Stop the bleeding by applying alum, cigarette ash (be sure it is cool!), baking soda or even powdered sugar. Then wash the area with soap and water and apply a skin lubricant. The same condition of the ears has been attributed to frostbite, something which occurs very easily if Dals are left outside too long on a cold day or night. The ears have poor circulation, with many small blood vessels close to the surface, and can become frostbitten easily, especially around the edges, which begin to have a "leathery" look.

A bath from time to time will keep the dog clean. One of the most beautiful elements of a Dalmatian is the striking contrast between the dark, rich spots and the bright white coat. One breeder suggests that the dog needs to be kept clean so the white can be appreciated. A Dalmatian coat will shed dirt and return to its bright color remarkably well, but a bath in the rainy season also helps keep that shed dirt off your carpets and furniture. They do not take long to dry — a brisk rub with a towel is enough to nearly dry them completely. In many cases, they can simply be wiped down with a wet cloth to get off dirt and mud after a romp in a spring mud puddle! One breeder recommends simply putting a dirty dog in a crate for about an hour with a large towel in the bottom. When he comes out, the coat will be clean and the towel can be washed.

Due to skin problems in the breed several of our breeders mention bathing with a very mild shampoo, cut in half with water to avoid a concentration which may be difficult to wash out. Rinsing is very important, since soap left in the coat can cause irritation. Use tepid water for bathing and rinsing. This way you keep the pores closed and bacteria may have a harder time entering the hair follicle. Use a washcloth around the sensitive areas of the top of the head and face. Dry the coat with the lay of the hair. One breeder recommends against using any human hair care product as the chemical balance is different for dogs than it is for humans. Several breeders recommend an aloe-based shampoo for dogs, and there are several good ones on the market. It goes without saying that you should never use bar soap or dishwashing detergent on your Dalmatian.

In adult dogs, ears should be checked and cleaned. As with any of the drop-eared breeds, dirt and infections can be caught in the ear canal where light and air does not reach. If the ear has an odor, is red or painful to the touch, or if the dog rubs his ears or shakes his head, or carries it cocked to one side, the ears are probably infected. Fungus infections may be a problem in humid climates. If odor or other indications of infection appear, consult your vet for medication. The periodic use of a few drops of ear wash will help prevent infections.

Ear mites may need treatment. Watch for odor in the ear area, or black "dirt" in the ear canal. If your dog has fleas, he probably also has ear mites. These conditions can easily be cured with a little time and low cost treatment. There are several good over-the-counter ear mite treatments which can be used if the black "dirt" appears. There are also a number of companies making good, all-natural ear cleaners which help to prevent ear mites and fleas and which help keep the ears clean, thereby preventing infection before it starts.

Always provide toys and chew items.

For most dogs, nails generally wear down with activity, especially if your Dalmatian gets lots of exercise. If you hear the nails clicking on the floor, or if they appear to be especially long, they should be cut back. Show breeders keep the nails of their dogs very short as this keeps the dog "up on his feet" and keeps pads from splaying out, especially as the dog grows and develops. Many of our breeders prefer to grind down nails rather than cut them especially if the nails are black, which make it almost impossible to see how far out the quick (or inner pulp) grows. When the quick is cut, it will bleed, sometimes profusely. Grinding is a little slower but the grinder creates enough heat to cauterize the quick as it shortens the nail and prevents bleeding. Dogs usually respond better to grinding than cutting. Begin to grind your puppy's nails early to get him used to it, and you will have less problem with his feet spreading out. By the time he is an adult, he will be used to the process and give you less trouble than if you wait until he is an adult before you try it for the first time.

Bronzing or Blackening — This is a passing problem and is neither associated with poor quality dogs or health or skin problems. The dense black or liver of the spots will sometimes "rust" out when it is time for the coat to be shed. This lightening, or losing color at the tip of the hair shaft, gives the black dogs a "bronze" (or brownish) overtone, and the livers a somewhat lighter, washed out appearance. Once shedding is complete, the dark rich color will return with the new hair.

Blackening is the opposite of bronzing and occurs only in the liver dogs. The liver spot color darkens to almost a black on most of the body. Since blackening is least likely to affect the ears and head, the dog looks to have both black and brown spotting, which is a major fault in the breed. Sometimes dogs have been disqualified in the show ring as tri-colors because of this phenomenon. This condition will pass when the new coat comes in, and it is sometimes best not to show a dog in blackening condition.

SHOW GROOMING

Dalmatians are easy to groom for the show ring. They are basically a wash-and-wear dog, needing only a good bath and brushing. Before showing, whiskers will be trimmed off, and the hair along the back of the leg, under the front area, along the ears and tail is usually trimmed to give a cleaner line. A Dal who has been living as a pet or playing in the yard can become a show dog in just a few minutes in terms of grooming.

SOCIALIZATION

With the Dalmatian, we have included socialization again under the "care" section because it is so important. Experiences and environments that challenge the curiosity and intelligence of the puppy are a necessary part of his development and mental health. He needs plenty of human contact and exposure to all sorts of common, everyday things, different sights, sounds and textures. It is necessary to his well-being that you pay attention to this need and provide it for him as he develops.

SHELTER

The Dalmatian is **NOT** a weather resistant dog. They do not tolerate extreme temperatures well. Since Dals like and need human contact, most are house dogs. They will play outside in bad weather and will even romp in the snow, but they need a warm, clean place to come in, dry off and settle into. Heat stroke is a problem if temperatures become too high. It is better to assume that the Dalmatian will be a house dog than to plan to keep him in a kennel or a doghouse. **NEVER, NEVER** keep him chained to a tree or doghouse.

FEEDING

Remember that feeding a dog is a little like feeding a baby. There are dozens of schools of thought, and thousands of dollars spent by dog food companies to develop, research and market their food. These high quality foods are complete and do not need to be supplemented with vitamins or other nutrients.

Many of our breeders recommended dry dog food because it gives the puppy a chance to chew and strengthen his teeth. This chewing will help take the place of the shoes

and corners of cabinets and save some of your sanity. It also keeps the teeth clean on older dogs and reduces the number of times in the dog's life you will need to take him to the veterinarian for a dental cleaning. Today, breeders are generally recommending that the protein level of dog food stay below 26%. Since most canned dog foods are 32% protein or higher, a diet which relies heavily on canned foods can cause stress on kidneys and other organs which become overloaded with very high protein levels. Dry dog food in the 23% protein range seemed to be the favorite of most of our breeders.

There are a number of excellent foods on the market. We suggest you talk to your breeder about what your dog has been eating. A puppy should be fed three to four times a day when he is very young, gradually decreasing the feedings to two by the time he is six months old, and an adult dog needs to eat only once a day. A puppy will eat almost as much as an adult dog.

Some of our breeders recommend free feeding, where the food is left in front of the dog all day and he feeds at will. Some days he may eat a lot, and some days he may eat almost nothing at all. Free-fed dogs, contrary to popular belief, are not necessarily overweight, as they tend to pace themselves and eat at whatever pattern nature suggests. When a dog is in good weight, you should not be able to feel the vertebrae along the backbone, but the dog should still have some definition in his body and loins.

It is especially important not to let a puppy put on too much weight, as it is hard on hips, joints and future health. Look at the recommended quantity on the dog food package for the weight of your dog.

Some dog foods have more bulk than others. Before you can say how much food a dog should eat each day, you must know if it is a high bulk or a low volume dog food. The obvious advantage to the low volume dog foods is that they also produce less waste to clean up. High bulk dog foods are viewed by some breeders as being inferior because they contain filler. Others feel the bulk is good for the dog's digestive system. Package guidelines for the individual food should be followed.

PARASITES

Although we have mentioned fleas in the Health chapter, the problem is so widespread that it bears mentioning again. A number of so-called skin problems are no more than reactions to fleas. People often tend to ignore a flea problem until the dog has developed obvious skin problems. Just because you don't see a flea doesn't mean that they aren't there. If you see black specks on your dog, usually at the point of the shoulder, at the base of the tail or on the stomach or chest, he has a flea problem. Regular spraying of the house, yard and dog will keep the problem under control. Some of our breeders recommend using flea dip, diluted according to the package directions, in a pump spray bottle. This homemade spray is usually much cheaper than regular sprays and is much easier to use than dipping the dog which requires a very large tub and a lot of water because of the size of the Dalmatian.

Worming is another health maintenance issue. Puppies pick up things in their mouths, just as babies do, and the possibility of picking up worms is almost constant if they are anywhere another dog has been. Especially in southeastern climates where parasites are a problem, pups should be wormed by the breeder, and again with each shot. After that, worming should be done on a regular basis, depending on your area and climate conditions. Yearly DHLP shots and rabies shots according to your state regulations are also part of dog care.

Heartworms are a problem across the country by now. There are a number of different types of medications for prevention. Treatment of an infected dog is costly and stressful on the dog. Prevention is much easier. When the dog goes in for his yearly health care and shots, he should be wormed and checked for heartworm. Ask your local vet what he recommends for treatment of heartworm in your area.

TRAINING

*I*f you are going to own a Dalmatian, take on the responsibility of training him from the beginning. As a responsible member of the community, it is your duty to be sure your dog does not contribute to a negative image of the breed. No matter how nice the temperament, the Dalmatian is a large, energetic dog and, without proper training and socialization, may be difficult to contain. The mental health of your dog depends on the type and consistency of training you give him. As with a child, this is his character you are molding. To a large extent, how well he fits into your family when he is an adult depends on the values you instill in him as a puppy and young adult.

Begin with a well-socialized puppy, one who has spent enough time with his litter and his dam to have acquired natural early socialization. This is a must, and lack of it is difficult to make up. The early socialization put in by the breeder promotes his attitude toward humans, his bond with them, and his acceptance of them as the "leader of his pack."

Time is a necessary ingredient. If you turn him out in a run or in the backyard and never have time for him, he will become wild and uncontrollable. Dalmatians love their families and need time to develop a bond. Quality time is no substitute for quantity! Though the quality of the time you spend with him is important, you also need to be sure there is enough of it so he does not feel alone.

Puppies have short attention spans. They need to be talked to, touched, petted and educated. It takes time, and lots of it, to build a lasting and loving companion, a friend that will understand your feelings and emotions, a protector, a confidant.

All breeders will recommend that Dalmatians receive basic obedience training at about six months of age. If possible, puppy kindergarten classes are advised. They teach the owner basic control skills for the new puppy. Dals can be quite bossy and stubborn, and it is important for the owner to be the dominant personality early in the relationship. The basic obedience should include sit, lay down, stay in the sit or down position until released, walk sensibly on a leash and come when called. The advantage to a class is that it allows the dog to learn in an environment with other dogs and distractions instead of an isolated, home situation and thus makes him more solid and stable when he is out.

Never try to dominate a Dalmatian physically. Dalmatians do best with motivational training, with short, frequent training sessions and with a variety of tasks which are kept interesting and challenging to the dog. But it is important to establish limits early. Be clear in your expectations and praise his positive behavior.

Be sure the early experiences are positive. If a Dalmatian is teased by children, for example, he may not be at ease with children later in his life. This is not the result of poor breeding or temperament, but a learned and developed behavior which is the natural product of bad experiences in the dog's early life.

The dam begins the puppy's training in the whelping box. When she is displeased with his behavior she will growl, shoving him with her muzzle and rolling him onto his back (the submissive behavior for dogs) or snapping at him if the behavior continues. Like his mother, a voice of displeasure, a sharply barked command, or a stern verbal reprimand will produce the desired effect in most cases. Begin with the command "NO," which roughly means, "Whatever you are doing, stop it!" In some cases, your pup may already have a rough knowledge of that command by the time he arrives at your home. If not, be sure it is the first thing you teach him.

Our breeders differ on discipline. Some think that a smack on the bottom is better than a finger on the nose, feeling that a rap on the nose will make the dog hand shy. Talk to your breeder before your pup comes home as to how to handle the rules and discipline. It is best to continue with the technique used by the breeder, especially for the first month or so until the pup develops and matures a little. In any case, the command and the reprimand should be short, firm and non-abusive. The idea is to stop the undesirable behavior, not to intimidate the dog.

Firm verbal commands and consistent, fair treatment should be the goal. People who are confident and stable in their own personalities will raise a dog which is confident and stable. If you are flighty or nervous, the Dalmatian is probably not the breed for you. Constant nagging and drawn-out punishment only confuses a dog and makes him resentful instead of sensitive to when you are displeased. Remember also that in order to make it important to him that he pleases you, he must KNOW when he pleases you. *Praise is an important and necessary ingredient.*

One trick is to outmaneuver the dog so that you never get into direct confrontation. Switching a favorite toy for a shoe you do not wish the puppy to chew gives you the shoe, and keeps you from simply pulling the shoe away from him. It is natural that the puppy will feel that the shoe is a prize, and he will try to take it back as a natural reaction. Or, he may mistake the action for a game. Dalmatians love to play games and he will naturally try to take it back. If you say "NO," take the shoe and give him the toy, he will learn the lesson, and be sidetracked to the toy instead of concentrating on getting the prize back.

Remember that chewing is a normal behavior for pups. They will taste test anything from rocks to furniture to wallpaper. Close supervision is a must. Never leave the pup alone. Provide him with toys and chew items which are his. And finally, try some of the products which are on the market that are designed to impart a bad taste to chairs, upholstery and other items you want the pup to stay away from. Success with these products has been mixed, but it never hurts to try and some reports have been successful.

Chewing and shredding are part of puppy play behavior. Early training, confining him when you are not around and not letting the pup get bored are all essential to raising a well adjusted dog. You will also need a lot of patience and understanding to get through the puppy stage!

Along the same lines, one breeder suggests a pile of sand or dirt in an old whiskey barrel placed in the back yard gives the young adult Dalmatian a place of his own to dig. If you start with a bone (or something which attracts the pup), half buried in the dirt or sand, he will get the idea.

Learning his name is another early lesson. The puppy has probably learned to come to a general puppy call for food, or to come in for the evening. Simply continue that by calling his name when you feed him. Although some of our breeders do not believe in treats to reward behavior, many others feel that this is a perfectly natural and acceptable practice. As long as the treat is accepted with proper control, not snapped out of the hand of the handler, it seems reasonable to many that the dog should get a reward for proper behavior.

Next, a puppy should learn to walk on a leash early in his life. The idea of trying to leash train a full-grown Dalmatian is much more daunting than trying to leash train a full-grown Toy Poodle, for example! Put the collar on the puppy and simply let him walk around. Some puppies will be convinced that they cannot move another inch until the collar comes off, while others are not concerned in the slightest and take little notice of what is hanging around their neck. Attach the leash, and simply follow the dog around for a while, going where he wants to go. You can increase your command over the situation by talking,

playing, or offering a treat to change the puppy's direction, or to make him follow you. Be sure that the lessons are short, and that he can always succeed in achieving what you want to teach him that day.

Never quit on a bad note, but don't continue to fight a losing fight. If he will not follow you, reconstruct the exercise so that you are asking him to do something you can get him to do. Then praise his efforts and quit for the day. Always break the task down into small parts that he can understand and make it as fun as possible for a very young puppy.

Dals generally love any type of activity where they can show off. One breeder says the main reason people don't see more Dals in obedience trials is that their intelligence makes them bored with the repetitive training necessary for the ring. She swore that they wait until they are "on stage" in the ring with the judge and the audience watching before deciding to do something just for laughs. Dals seem to greatly enjoy both agility and flyball competitions, perhaps because these activities are not quite as disciplined and structured as the obedience show ring.

By the time he is six months old and ready for adult obedience classes, he should have some understanding of basic commands such as his name, "No," how to walk on a leash, and how to know when you are pleased and when you are not pleased. If you have taken him out and about on a regular basis, the noise, confusion and other dogs in the obedience class should not frighten him. Obedience classes in some areas of the country are crowded and there may be a waiting list. Breeders often recommend that you investigate these classes immediately upon purchasing a puppy so that you will be at the top of the waiting list by the time the puppy is ready to begin formal training.

Remember, never let a puppy do anything you do not want a full-grown Dalmatian to do. Behaviors which are cute on a Miniature Pinscher, or even a Cocker Spaniel, may not be as cute in a sixty-pound dog. Jumping up to say "Hello" is one example. Another is running after people and grabbing at their feet. Discourage these behaviors while the puppy is young with firm, immediate correction.

Dalmatians are not especially difficult to housetrain. Especially if they have been kept clean and in a large enough place to have a "living area" and a "potty" area, they are likely to have taken the first steps in housetraining before they arrive at your home. This is a critical point in the life of a puppy, because it sets the tone for your appreciation of the dog. A dog which is not housetrained is no fun for anyone.

Successful housebreaking depends on understanding the instinctive and biological behaviors of dogs. There are three basic factors: **timing, location and equipment.**

Timing — There are certain times when a puppy must eliminate, and will eliminate regardless of where he is. It is therefore necessary that the human in charge of housetraining be available to let the dog in and out at those times. **After he sleeps,** a pup will wake up, totter away from his sleeping area, and squat. **After he plays,** or sometimes while he is playing, since active play can trigger the need to eliminate, he will need to go. **After eating** or drinking, a puppy will need to go outside.

Location — This can provide a cue for your puppy to eliminate. **Dogs mark their territory.** This is instinctive. If a puppy comes to think of the extra bedroom or the unused living room as "his," he may mark it to keep others out. Always keep an eye on him. By getting him to eliminate in an area you feel comfortable with, you will get him to "mark" that territory.

If any **odor** is left in the place where the puppy has had an accident, it will trigger the use again. Even when you clean it completely with ordinary household disinfectants, you may still be leaving an odor the dog can smell. This is why people sometimes replace carpet in a pet stained area, only to have the new dog use the same spot. The flooring under the carpet may have become soiled, and the chemical decomposition of the waste products is what actually causes the odor. There are a number of enzyme-based cleaners which do a good job bonding with the decaying waste, and they actually eliminate odor more effectively than simply using a typical disinfectant cleaning solution.

Finally, **habit** brings the pup back to the same spot. This is especially true if the spot is easily accessible and out of sight of the person who is most likely to scold him for his behavior.

Equipment — A **crate** is a must. We have already mentioned crate training, and a crate is useful for a number of reasons. It gives the pup or dog a place which is "his" and allows him to have part of his home with him when he travels. (See the chapter on Traveling.) It keeps the pup or young adult from causing damage when you are gone. Finally, because he naturally does not want to soil his sleeping quarters, the pup will try to wait until he can get out to another area. He may learn to pace or bark to get your attention and announce that he wants to go out. You should be sure he is not confined for periods of time longer than he can comfortably contain himself. When you take him out of the crate, be sure you take him directly outside and praise him when he does eliminate in the desired area. This routine will help set a pattern and encourage his behavior.

Keep a puppy confined when you cannot watch him to help house train him and keep him from developing bad habits.

Since the Dalmatian is a curious dog by nature, some owners report success with a **bell** tied to the door. When the dog investigates the bell, let him out. When you let him out, ring the bell. In this way the dog quickly relates the ringing of the bell with going outside and learns the signal to go out.

Dog doors are often useful. Dogs learn to use these at an early age, and will almost naturally learn to go out to relieve themselves.

Finally, a **simple leash**, long enough to allow the pup some room to roam will do a number of things to promote housetraining. If you use a lightweight leash indoors to keep the puppy near, you are more likely to notice the restless behavior which signals is need to go out. And it will keep your dog from wandering off into another room. With the leash, the pup is more likely to begin to signal to go out as soon as he gets the idea because he cannot simply wander off.

Some other suggestions: Do not free feed the dog. A set schedule of both feeding and exercise makes housetraining easier. Always feed, then take the dog out for exercise to set a routine which promotes housetraining. Talk to the dog so he gets used to the excitement of going outside. Always use the same words and tone of voice so he learns to associate that with going outside. Praise him when he eliminates where you want him to, and always use the same door to let him in and out so he gets used to going to that door to go outside. Select a place outside and always take your pup directly to the same spot. Don't walk him aimlessly around looking for a place which "suits" him. If you take your pup for a walk for exercise, always do it after a successful housetraining trip to an area of your choice, not before. And most importantly, limit his area when in the house by using a crate, closing doors and putting up baby gates. Never allow a new dog or puppy access to the entire house.

One final note pointed out by one of our breeders is that puppies learn by repetition and copying. This can mean copying an older dog. If the other dog is clean and well behaved, the pup will copy that behavior. But if the pup sees another dog digging, tearing up the house or backing off and treating strangers with apprehension, he will learn to do the same. Be sure that the behavior your pup learns from an older dog is positive, and keep your puppy away from the older dog if the older dog is apt to be exhibiting behavior you do not want copied by the pup.

SHIPPING AND TRAVEL

*T*he first opportunity a puppy has to travel is when he goes to his new home. In some cases, you may not be able to find the kind of dog you are looking for locally. It is more important to find the right dog than to locate something fast or close. If you have a choice of driving eight or ten hours or flying a dog, flying may be preferable. Although some of our breeders are very much against flying, many report that puppies travel very well, and several indicated that they felt a flight was less stressful on the pup — who will probably go to sleep with the sound of the engines — than a drive in a car which may be a longer trip, with more temperature and water changes, strange potty stops where the pup may be exposed to viruses, lack of exercise and motion which may cause car sickness. It is very common for pups to get car sick and not get air sick.

Flying a puppy in is relatively easy. According to airline regulations, a puppy may not fly until it is eight weeks old. Shipping should take place after the first set of shots has been given. The cost is usually $70-$110 for the flight, and $25-$55 for the crate. A dog may not ship if the temperature is below 30°, or higher than 90°. If the pup goes freight, you may pay for the flight and even the crate (if you purchase it from the airlines) collect, at the time you pick up your pup at the airport. Airlines use top-of-the line crates but there are several good, less expensive crates on the market which are still safe and airline approved, but at half the cost. The puppy will ship in the smallest crate possible because freight is charged not only by weight, but by dimensions. Therefore, the crate you use to ship the puppy will not be useful for a full-grown Dalmatian which will need a much larger crate. The breeder will drop the puppy off at the freight office of the airline, and you will pick him up at the freight office.

If the pup flies counter-to-counter, the freight must be paid when the dog is put on the plane. The advantage to this method is that the temperature restrictions are much less rigid since the puppy is hand carried to the plane and loaded with the baggage. Less time is needed between flights if the dog must make a connecting flight, and the dog is dropped off at the ticket counter and picked up with oversized baggage. However, there is a size and weight limit on this type of shipping and only smaller puppies will qualify.

On the Boston Commons in the summer.

Although there are some stories of dogs being mishandled or dying during shipping, one breeder says she has shipped dogs over half of a million air miles over the years, and never had a problem. We could not find a single breeder who had directly had a real trauma with airlines. While some breeds of dogs have breathing or respiration problems which make them poor shipping risks, Dalmatians will generally settle in for the ride and enjoy the experience.

If you have picked your pup up at the airport, bring him directly home; do not use that opportunity to visit friends and show him off. He needs to see his new home, have time and quiet to get adjusted, and get food and water. Although the airlines require food and water dishes, most breeders will not send food or water with the pup. A full stomach can lead to airsickness, and water bowls tip as the crate is carried and leave the bedding wet and cold. Bring the pup home, let him inspect the new area and give him a bed, food and water immediately. With a full stomach and a little quiet, he will settle in a short time. Don't expect him to be himself right away. It will probably take a day or two for him to settle in and become the normal, active puppy he was when he left his litter.

The next time your dog will have a chance to fly might be on vacation with you. Check the dog in as excess luggage and it will fly with you for a minimal cost. If you are not traveling with your dog, shipping a full-grown Dalmatian, usually in a #400 or #500 crate, may be expensive. Be prepared to pay $100 to $160 for a one-way trip. For that reason, bitches being bred to dogs out of the area often make use of frozen semen, which can go in overnight mail or be shipped counter-to-counter as medical supplies.

Although dogs may not travel on trains, they do adapt easily to new places if they have been raised properly, and they can become good, solid travelers. They travel well in motor homes for a change of pace family vacation, and Dalmatians are usually happy see new surroundings. Long hikes in the wilderness or walks in a new city can be of interest to them!

Traveling with a puppy takes a little extra time and energy. If you are traveling by car with a puppy, take a few precautions to help make the trip easier. Do not feed him for an hour or so before you leave. Many pups get car sick — throw up or drool constantly — in a moving car. One breeder suggests feeding the pup a couple of gingersnaps before travel to help carsickness. (Pups who get carsick generally outgrow it by the time they are six months old.) Take him for a walk right before departure so that he has every opportunity to relieve himself while he still has the chance. Take along a box, bed or crate that he is used to so that something familiar will accompany him, much like bringing along a stuffed animal or blanket for a child. Don't let him travel with his head out the window, because he can get grit or wind in his eyes and because he does not have the intelligence to realize how fast the car is traveling and he may suddenly try to jump out. Stop every few hours to let him get a drink of water, get some exercise and relieve himself. But be sure to keep him on a leash so that he does not dart out in front of a car, run off and get lost or approach a strange dog. Never let your pup approach a strange dog. If the strange dog challenges him, and the pup becomes defensive, the other dog may react too quickly for you to prevent serious injury to the puppy.

If you are using hotels, most of our breeders offer one word of advice: CRATE. Crate train your dog, and bring the crate on vacation with you. Some hotels will accept a crated dog, while they have learned not to accept dogs which may be left on their own in hotel rooms, bored, upset, and ready to do damage that these perfect pets would never think of doing at home. A crate is not unpleasant to a dog. For him, it is a part of his home which has come with him and gives him a feeling of stability. The crate can help him stay calm and get some sleep while you go out to dinner or to see sights where a dog may not be allowed.

A hotel room with a crate is certainly safer and better than locking him in a hot car.

If you are traveling with your dog, be sure to bring bowls for food and water. Some breeders recommend bringing not only food from home, but water so the dog does not get an upset stomach from the change in water. Other breeders say Dalmatians are not sensitive to water changes and there is no need to carry along water from home. Other helpful items to travel with are Pepto Bismol tablets in case he gets hold of something that gives him diarrhea, Dramamine for carsickness (especially if it is a young dog who has not ridden in a car often), Benadryl for insect bites, and flea spray, especially if you are near the beach. Having these things with you when you need them can take some of the stress out of travel.

In hot weather, a crate is a necessity. **Never** leave a dog in the car, but if you are going somewhere such as a picnic or a baseball game, take the crate out of the car, place it in the shade, and the dog can safely be left without worrying about overheating. Heat stroke is one of the leading causes of death in well-loved dogs — be careful during summer months.

Dalmatians enjoy outdoor activities, but they do not tolerate either extreme in temperature. Their short coat and lean body build do not give them much protection in cold. They are better off in the house during the cold of winter or the heat of summer.

If you are traveling and intend to leave the dog at home, you have three choices: you can kennel your dog, leave him in the care of a friend or relative, or set up some kind of care for him at your home. A kennel is the safest and easiest way to care for your dog when you are away. Some Dalmatians do not care for strangers and some of our breeders feel they do better in a kennel where strangers leave them alone than in the home of a friend or family member they do not know well. Other pets already in the home may also be a problem and may not enjoy the visit from the newcomer. By contrast, they will survive a kennel trip well if it is a reputable, clean kennel and they can have their own area and the chance to stay alone until their owner returns.

If you are counting on someone coming into the house to feed and care for your dog, be sure that they are reliable. Many areas of the country have professional "pet-sitters." These people come into the home, check on pets and care for them, and keep an eye on the house at the same time. Professional pet-sitters offer the advantage of keeping the dog at home where he feels comfortable. Also, having someone in and out of the house, and with the dog there to watch out for intruders, burglary may be deterred. However, a bored Dalmatian, without human contact for several days in a row, may become destructive even though he is usually well mannered. How practical it is to leave the dog at home instead of at a boarding kennel depends on how secure your yard (or the area where the dog is to be housed) may be. If there is a yard or pool man going in and out, for example, there is a possibility that the dog will slip out. If the fencing is not secure, or the shelter not good, this is not a good alternative. Above all, the reliability of the pet-sitter may be a problem. Friends, or sitters that are not well recommended, may be too busy to come by on a regular basis, and the dog may be at risk because a problem may go undetected. Be sure the pet sitter is experienced with dogs and knows your dog well enough to tell if there is a problem.

BREEDING YOUR DOG -
WHY THIS MIGHT NOT BE SUCH A GOOD IDEA!

*N*ow that you have your dog, you may entertain the idea of breeding it. If you read one of the larger books on the breed or one of the many dog books that promote breeding, it will discuss genetics and how to build a whelping box, and it will make it sound easy. On the other hand, breeders and breed associations will say that "you should not breed your dog." That makes it sound like an ethical decision on a high moral plane and you may be tempted to simply say, "But I just want one litter; what could it hurt?" Here is probably the most honest evaluation of why this may be one of the many times in life when something LOOKS better on the outside than it does when you actually TRY it.

Have you ever gone somewhere and seen a WONDERFUL layout of model trains or a large doll house? The hobby looked easy and fascinating. You may have even gone home and bought a small doll house kit, or a starter set of trains. Then you began to discover just how much time and money really went into this simple looking project. You needed space to work on the project, and space to set it up. You needed special tools and materials you had never worked with before, and they were all expensive. You had to spend time shopping for the right pieces of the right size so that it all went together and they were expensive. Very quickly you found that this seemingly simple setup was going to cost you hours and hours of your life and hundreds of dollars just to get off to a good start. And when you put together the first pieces, it was a boring, poor substitute for the intricate, fascinating setup you had seen. In the end, you gave up on it, losing the money you had invested in the train set which is now on a shelf in the garage, or the doll house which still sits without those hundreds of maddening little shingles pasted to the roof! In short, your time and money were not well spent unless you found it to be something you were interested in to the point where you became involved and dedicated!

Dalmatians are born white. This litter of one day old puppies will grow rapidly and will need supervision and care until they go to their new homes. This litter is unusually large, with fourteen pups.

Like all hobbies, there is much more to dog breeding than first meets the eye. Enthusiasts put time and money into this, just as with any hobby. The result that looks simple is the product of careful planning and investment. To do it with any less than that kind of planning will result in something far short of the goal, which is a waste of your time and money. Even a single litter can consume much more time and money than you ever imagined on the way into the project.

In 1995, 12,596 litters of Dalmatians were registered with AKC, while individual animals being registered numbered 36,714. Statistically, this means that only about three pups are registered per litter, while the size of a litter as reported by our breeders is six to ten pups. Every year there are thousands of puppies which are eligible for registration but which for one reason or another are not registered. Not only are there a lot of pet-quality Dalmatians out there, some of whom are being bred, but there are a lot of unregistered dogs bearing some resemblance to a Dalmatian being bred in backyards and flooding the market with poor quality pups. If an owner does not care enough about his dog or think it is important to register the dog in the first place, common sense says that he will not put much care into the planning of the breeding if he decides to have a litter. While he may take care of the bitch, he will not be well-educated in how to socialize the pups in their early development, how to select a puppy which will fit your home, or how to predict which health or temperament problems may occur! This also means that should you decide to produce a litter without proper dedication to the project, you will be competing for the bottom-end homes for your puppies in this very flooded market. With that kind of population, it is no wonder that the breed has suffered in quality, health and temperament. All Dalmatians are simply NOT alike!

It also means that, realistically speaking, the nearly thirteen thousand litters will produce nearly one hundred thousand Dalmatian puppies — and about ten to twelve **thousand** will be deaf! **BE CAREFUL WHERE YOU BUY YOUR DOG AND DON'T PLAY WITH THESE STATISTICS BY BREEDING YOUR DOG UNLESS YOU KNOW THE ODDS OF PRODUCING DEAF PUPS AND HOW TO SPOT THEM.** If you truly want to breed, even after reading this chapter, find an experienced breeder to help you and breed only good quality, tested bitches to good quality, tested dogs. Even then, you must be prepared to test your litter for hearing and put down those pups who are deaf.

Most people decide to breed their dog for one of the following reasons:

A) It looks like easy money. Call a few breeders, find out the price of pups and the number of pups in a litter, and the profit doesn't look bad. But remember, you are playing the *Kibbles and Bits Slot Machine.* You may make money on a litter here and there, but there is a greater potential to lose money, sanity, friends and routine. The odds are better at Las Vegas. How much stress is it worth to you to make a few dollars? How many nice things are in your home that you would prefer not to see with tooth marks? And like any new business venture, there is ALWAYS investment before there is profit. How much are you willing to invest before you have a payoff? Expect to spend at least $1,500 to $2,500 to raise and sell a litter. Most dedicated breeders estimate that a litter will cost them $3,000 to $3,500 to raise!

By two weeks old, the spots are beginning to come up, eyes start to open, and pups begin to move around — and get into trouble! This is a more typical litter with eight pups.

B) People think that it would be a wonderful experience for the children. But the kids will play with the pups for a few days and then go back to Nintendo or outside to play ball, depending on their interests. A litter of eight-week-old pups is too young to have manners enough to stay away from Nintendo controls, but too small to play outside with the kids! In the end, the kids may find the pups more annoying than interesting. It is like having six to ten toddlers around the house. One of our breeders remembers several times when her children took pups out of the puppy area, then got interested in something else and left unhousetrained pups prying into every corner of the house unsupervised!

Remember that whelping may occur at 3 a.m.; will the kids want to be up all night? The gory part of whelping repulses most children. And how will you explain to them that one or two of the pups may have to be put down because they cannot hear? Can you explain to them that this condition — unlike that of the nice kid they may know who is deaf and uses sign language — involves deteriorating neurons in the brain and will likely lead to a dog who cannot cope, even if he has a very loving family? If you want the kids to see the joy of birth, BUY A VIDEO. It's cheaper, more informative, and in the end the house smells better!

Dalmatians are usually good mothers, like this bitch, but sometimes there is great stress for a family pet to be torn between her desire to be with her human family and the instinct to be with her pups.

C) You may decide you want a second dog. The chances are you will **not** get another just like your dog. Friends and family have said they also wanted a dog. But frequently friends who have repeatedly said, "If you ever breed Freckles, we want a pup," will be the first to tell you AFTER the litter is eight weeks old and you have asked them when they are going to get their puppy, that they "really can't take a puppy this time, but for sure the next time you breed her!" Besides, most of these people will want a puppy for free, and why should you invest time and money just to get them a free dog?

D) There may be no decision at all. A neighborhood male jumped the fence. (Yes, even six footers have been known to be scaled.) The bitch slipped out past the kids when she was in season. No one realized that she was in season. The list goes on and on. It is much easier to get an accidental breeding than you can ever imagine. Mixed litters are the hardest to get rid of, and you have all the disadvantages of raising a litter with none of the advantages of producing a nice puppy, or being able to sell it. For this reason, we highly recommend that you SPAY ANY BITCH YOU DID NOT BUY FOR THE EXPRESS PURPOSE OF BREEDING OR SHOWING.

If you bought your dog as a pet, you may find that you have a limited registration, which means that your pups are not eligible for registration. The breeder, with his knowledge of the gene pool for the breed in general and his line in particular, may have priced your dog as a pet and found a pet home for her because for some reason he did not feel that puppies should be produced from her.

When you consider breeding your dog, think about some very important factors. First, did you buy a nice quality dog from a good breeder? Is this a dog the breeder himself would want to breed? If the answer is "NO," don't breed your dog just to get a litter of puppies. This kind of breeding lowers the quality of the Dalmatian and gives the breed a bad name. If you did not make it clear that you were looking for a breeding bitch at the time of purchase, the chances are that your bitch is not of breeding quality. This goes back to the necessity of making it very clear *what* you want the dog for at the time of purchase. There may be hidden genetic problems that the breeder knows are in your dog — ones that will not affect her life and health, but which may appear in her puppies. The breeder may not have explained this to you because you said all you wanted was a pet. As long as *your* dog was not affected by it, there was no reason for the breeder to go into it. But if you breed the dog, they will surely appear again and then *you* are the breeder who has to deal with the problem. Then *you* will have puppy buyers coming back to you with a problem with your puppies.

How will you handle it?

Second, even though there are a lot of dogs in the newspaper every week, remember that with all of the Dals out there, it may not be as easy as it looks to sell the pups. It is one thing to look at a litter of eight pups and say to yourself, "Even at $300 each, that is $2,100!" and another to reap that kind of profit. The road is filled with pitfalls, chewed furniture, expenses that add up like a city street repair budget, and more work than coaching a Little League team!

It may sound like a jackpot. You appear to do nothing and extra pocket money comes rolling in! But think about the expenses you incur. Pups need shots and worming. Even if your vet is very reasonable, $60 is the lowest you will pay for a litter of seven pups ($25 for the office call and $5 per pup).

Three and a half weeks old and pups are moving around, eating solid food, and showing some personality.

You have the expense of the puppy food and the additional food the bitch will require during the time she is carrying and nursing. You have to build or buy a box for whelping or she will pick the bed, a closet (after she has pulled all of the clothes off the hangers to make her own bed) or the middle of the flower bed.

Advertising in the local newspaper will run $20 to $40 per weekend. Count the number of Dalmatian ads in your newspaper. The odds are that you will not be able to sell the entire litter in one weekend. It will take you two or three *at best*. You will have to stay home to answer the phone, and you will have at least a dozen strangers coming to your home to see the pups, and many of them will simply be on an outing. Puppies are cute and there are the inevitable "window shoppers." The price of three or four pups will be needed JUST TO COVER THE EXPENSE YOU HAVE IN RAISING THE LITTER AND SELLING IT. The longer you have to keep the pups before selling them, the more you have invested in them in terms of time and money. All you have to do is start calling around the ads in local papers to see that the older the pups get, the more the price falls, as people panic over keeping a half dozen bouncing, boisterous, blundering pups for six months — ruining the house, the yard and all semblance of sanity! What will you do if you cannot find homes for them? How long will you keep them before dumping them at the animal shelter which will only add to the overpopulation of dogs? How will you explain **that** to the children?

In addition, there is the expense and trouble of the breeding itself. Either one pup or a stud fee is usually paid to the owner of the stud, even if he is a local dog. Stud fees on known dogs run around $400 and can run as high as $1,000 for a well known dog and many breeders will ask that the fee be paid at the time the breeding is made. This is six to eight weeks before the litter is born, and about four months before you can sell the pups. If you have picked a dog from some distance away, you will need to ship either the bitch or the semen. Shipping the frozen semen is easier, but then you must pay a vet, or someone who is authorized to make the breeding, to inseminate the bitch. Also consider the times you will try to breed, and the bitch will simply not become pregnant.

If you are breeding to a good stud, you will have to plan ahead to book the breeding. It is best to start the process *before* the bitch comes in season. You will need to send a copy of your bitch's pedigree and perhaps her picture to the owner of the stud for approval in most cases. When it is time for breeding, you will have to get a current brucellosis test. Although uncommon, brucellosis is a contagious disease which is usually sexually transmitted between dogs. It can be contagious to humans from handling the dogs during breeding or whelping, and there is some new evidence to show that it can also be transmitted between dogs through waste material. Rather than risk it, most breeders will require a current brucellosis certificate. A test from six months or a year before is not considered current. Many breeders will also require hip certification and BAER testing.

There are often problems with a sale. Someone buys a pup and it gets sick, and they want YOU to pay the vet bill. Or they can't keep it and want to bring it back. Someone brings in a virus, the litter gets sick and you have hundreds of dollars of vet bills —

it happens all the time. Even the best breeders have problems with a virus in a litter from time to time. Do you know how and where to get the pups tested for hearing? What will you do with a puppy you do not recognize as a deaf puppy until *after* it goes to its new home? Will you be willing to help new buyers and answer their questions even if it means that you have to call a mentor breeder to find out? Will you take the time and care to give a written contract and written instructions to new owners?

As the pups begin to move around, they may get out of their area and chew up furniture or kitchen cabinets. The force of a litter of wiggling, happy, uncontrollable seven-week-old puppies is enough to move baby gates and temporary pens, and to scratch up doors and cabinets. Outside, these little fellows will dig and chew up bushes unless you have a separate pen built for them. This may mean the expense of building some place to contain them between the time the bitch has had enough, and you can sell them. This could be the longest month of your life!

And winter puppies, inside because of the cold weather, will shred papers, take down barriers, and create literally several pounds of wet and soiled papers a day. Mopping and scraping smeared puppy poop will become a way of life! One of our breeders described puppies as "poop machines" eating three times a day, they will produce what seems to be their weight in wet, dirty papers every day! Certainly there are crates and cages called "puppy playpens" which do a very good job containing puppies and eliminate some of the mess. But they will run in the neighborhood of $140 each and will take up a space of about 4' X 4' in some inconvenient place in your home! And a large litter will have too many pups for one playpen, so you will need two.

In short, many people breed a litter because they think it is easy money, they want the "experience" of having a litter (which is a little like wanting to have the "experience" of juggling five bowling balls without dropping them on your foot!), and because they want the kids to have the fun of a litter. They may want a second dog and this looks like a way to get one for themselves, friends or family members.

By the time you add up expenses, it is cheaper to simply buy a nice second dog. One puppy is fun, two are a chore and four can be overwhelming if you are not set up for it and if you do not have the time to devote to it. Eight or ten can be a nightmare, making this the longest two or three months of your life. Breeders do this as a hobby. It interests them, and they have invested time and money — just as you would with any hobby that interests you — in finding the best way to handle pups. Every one of them has early disaster stories to tell.

And perhaps this is the time to mention that the odor of your home may change, and friends may be less inclined to visit. Whelping has a distinctive smell. Amniotic fluid is dark green, stains what it comes in contact with, and has a permeating fragrance. Although the bitch will clean up after the litter when they are very young, her housekeeping may be somewhat lax when they get older and start on solid food. One of our breeders says she bought a breadmaking machine so that the aroma of yeast and fresh bread would fill the house instead of the aroma of puppies!

Time is another thing you will need. Are you prepared to stay home when the bitch is ready to whelp? In accordance with Murphy's Law, the bitch is guaranteed to whelp in the middle of a dinner party, or on the day you have an important appointment — even if she has to be days early or days late to do it! The need for a Caesarean section can lead to even more time and expense, as much as $500. And you must be experienced enough to recognize when a bitch is in trouble and needs to go to the vet, and when things are progressing well even if it is a slow process. First time bitches are often poor or confused mothers who do not clean pups well, or who step on pups. You should always be present at a whelping, especially of a first time bitch, or risk losing pups and/or the dam. There are a tremendous number of health issues which may arise that may threaten both the bitch and pups, leading to vet expenses which can overwhelm you. Finally, bitches shed after they have a litter. Do not expect her to be in top condition for several months.

After they are born, you will need to start handling the pups from the beginning. Watch for poor nursers. Sometimes you will need to physically put a puppy — which is nursing slowly or getting shoved out of a big litter — on the teat and hold him on until he can get his fill. There is always the chance that one or more of the pups will need tube or bottle feeding at least as a supplement. There is the time you will need to take them to the vet for shots, and the time you will need to spend with them just getting them used to people and being handled. And there is the inevitable clean-up time. When the litter gets older, they will be glad to try to help you with these chores by eating the mop, broom or papers as you are trying to get the job done. This kind of help does not speed up the process. Pups need to be fed and cared for like babies, in the morning when you are late, and at night when you are tired.

You will need portable pens such as this one to allow the pups to get exercise when the weather is nice.

One of our breeders said, "The amazing thing about it is that when a mother sheep has baby sheep, the mother sheep takes care of them. When a mother horse has a baby horse, the mother horse takes care of it. But when a bitch whelps, YOU take care of them!"

If you truly are interested in breeding dogs, go to some shows, talk to breeders, do your homework for the next phase of your hobby, just as we have advised you throughout this book. Determine the style of dog you want to breed, the temperament you feel a Dalmatian should have, and the purpose you want your puppies to fill in their new homes. Consider that you will need to keep pups from time to time in order to see how well your breeding program is working. Do you have room for several adults?

Then, study the pedigrees to find out what bloodlines are most likely to produce the type of dog you want. Decide how you will determine if you are reaching your goal.

Puppies are very cute but...

Will you show them to check their conformation quality? Will you temperament test them, check on the pups after they have been placed in homes, use them as therapy dogs? What kind of homes will they fit into, and how will you sell them? What kind of guarantee will you offer new owners? How will you handle problems which may arise with new owners who are having a problem with their puppies? Do you have enough experience to be able to help them, or can you get the information from a mentor breeder?

From a practical standpoint, how will you handle the litter? Look at facilities of other breeders. Ask what kinds of equipment you will need. Can you find a good vet who is familiar with the breed and knows anything about whelping and caring for a litter? Where will you get help if something goes wrong? Do you have the time to socialize the puppies, and a clear idea of how you will do it?

We strongly advise finding a breeder who is willing to work with you as a mentor. They have the experience you will need to tap into and can give you advice along the way if things don't go as planned.

After you have thought out the project completely, do your first breeding. Like anything else, careful planning and forethought can save stress, money, grief and your home!

Some of our breeders recount how they got started. For many, it was a matter of seeing a dog they liked, investigating his lines, and finding the right person to help and advise them. Then they invested as much money as they could afford in the best bitch they could find. Sometimes this worked, but many of our breeders reported starting again and again until they got the right foundation stock, clear of problems and representing the ideal they had in mind for the breed. Some of the best advice comes from an old breeder who said, "Never get attached to a breeding bitch." If you have a pet or breeding or show quality, and she turns out to be a poor producer (and even top winners may not be good producers or good mothers), keep her, love her, BUT STOP BREEDING HER! If you wish to continue breeding, purchase another bitch.

There is a lot more to breeding than owning a pet. If you intend to do it, be sure that you do it as well as you can. This determination will provide you with the best possible chance of producing quality puppies and having happy new owners.

It's usually best to let a loving pet do what loving pets do best — take care of their human families!

SHOPPING ARCADE

THE FOLLOWING SECTION IS A SHOWCASE OF FINE COMPANIES WHO PRODUCE AND SELL PRODUCTS WHICH ARE OF INTEREST TO DALMATIAN OWNERS.

Many of these goods and services you will not find in the course of your normal shopping patterns. Those who are involved with dogs and dog shows are used to finding an abundance of these kinds of products at the many show vendors they see each weekend, but we know that many of our readers do not have the same opportunities. We hope that by presenting these companies to you here, it will make your life with your Dalmatian a little richer and easier. Please feel free to write us and let us know how you feel about this section, or this book in general. We encourage your comments and would like to hear from you. If at any time after publication you cannot make contact with a company listed in this section, or a breeder listed in the breeder sections, please contact Dace Publishing to get an updated number.

SHOPPING ARCADE

PET DOORS

Featuring the Energy Conserving Ultraseal Flap System. Available sizes: Small, Medium, Medium-Tall, Large, Large-Tall and X-Large. Easily installs in all types of doors, walls and sliding glass doors. Made in America. For information, discount coupons and nearest participating dealer, call today!

Call Toll Free 800·738·3677

PURE BRED PINS
In Sterling Silver

Hand & Hammer Silversmiths has created sterling silver jewelry of your favorite dog. Each lapel pin is handmade in sterling silver by craftsmen at Hand & Hammer. Sizes vary, approx. 1". $20 postpaid VA residents add 4 5/8 sales tax

Breeds: Airedale, Akita, Basset Hound, Beagle, Bichon Frise, Border Collie, Boston Terrier, Boxer, Bull Dog, Chihuahua, Chow, Cocker Spaniel, Collie, Dachshund, Dalmatian, Doberman, Fox Terrier, German Shepherd, Golden Retriever, Great Dane, Greyhound, Husky, Jack Russell, Labrador, Lhasa Apso, Maltese, Pekingese, Pembroke and Cardigan Corgi, Pomeranian, Poodle, Pug, Rottweiler, Shar-Pei, Schnauzer, Scottish Terrier, Shetland Sheepdog, Shih Tzu, Springer Spaniel, Westie, Yorkie.

Hand & Hammer Silversmiths
2610 Morse Lane, Woodbridge, VA 22192
Check, VISA, Mastercard
1-800-SILVERY

English bridle leather dog collars, leashes and accessories of exquisite character and style.

For a free catalog call
1-800-736-4746

The
Largest Pet Supply Catalog
in the industry,
owned & operated by practicing veterinarians
Dr. Race Foster & Dr. Marty Smith
Low prices on high quality vitamins, medications,
flea & tick products, toys, beds, treats & more....Over 130 pages!

Call for your FREE catalog!
1-800-323-4208
Ask for catalog code: #120/2014

SHOPPING ARCADE

PEDIGREE SEARCH!

CERTIFIED PEDIGREE - Extensive information now available on your Dalmatian's ancestry. Have it searched and handsomely documented on parchment with champions and titles in red, coat colors, whelp dates, and OFA's if available. Designed to make your dog's ancestry look superior in every detail. Includes work sheet to help answer your breeding questions. Mailed rolled ready for framing. Everyone admires. Perfect for breeding, buying, selling or simply displaying with pride of ownership! Money back satisfaction guaranteed.

5 generations: 63 dogs $20;   ✳ 6/127 $40; 7/254 $80

Easy order (610) 327-1309
or send copy of AKC registration to:

CANINE FAMILY TREE
PO BOX 756-DP6
Pottstown, PA 19464-0756

FREE CATALOG
We stock everything you need!
Cages, crates, beds, mats, leads, collars, shampoos and treats. We also carry a wide range of books.

We specialize in SHOW-TRAINING and PROFESSIONAL GROOMING Supplies.

We have many hard to find items in stock!

Write or Call today for your
FREE
CAR...
1617 Diam...
Virginia...
8...
in VA...
Most orders...

The Basic Guide To The Dalmatian
77990
636.7
D148

97696

DACE Publishing

P.O. Box 91
Ruckersville, VA 22968
(804) 985-3603

Dace Publishing is proud to present the *Basic Guide Breed Series*. With emphasis on the unique qualities of each breed, we present up-to-date information on style, health, temperament and suitability of each breed by interviewing breeders across the country.

Our titles include:

Basic Guide to the Labrador Retriever
Basic Guide to the Chinese Shar-Pei
Basic Guide to the Rottweiler
Basic Guide to the American Cocker Spaniel
Basic Guide to the Doberman Pinscher
Basic Guide to the Great Dane
Basic Guide to the Dalmatian
Basic Guide to the German Shepherd
Basic Guide to the Poodle
Basic Guide to the Dachshund

All Available at $9.95 plus shipping and handling.

Also available:
The Dalmatian Family Photo Album
This wonderful collection of photos from breeders across the country shows the Dalmatian at home, at work and at play. This simple story delights both child and adult alike.

64 pages, full color cover — $6.95

With **new titles currently under production.** Order directly, or **call for additional titles** which are being added all the time.

TO ORDER:
Title(s) X $9.95 each, plus $3.00 shipping and handling for up to three books, $5.00 for up to five books and $.35 for each additional book (Continental U.S.) VA res. add 4.5% sales tax.

Send name, address, phone number along with payment.
Payment by check, VISA, MC. Include name on card, number and expiration date.

OR CALL FOR DIRECT ORDERING —
Orders Only 1-888-840-DACE (3223)

Ch. Dalanna Moonlite Royal Mist

and

Jap/Am Ch. Centurion Cliffhanger

"Misty"

"Cliff"

Introduce:

Dalanna's Mark of Montazh

Pictured at 5 weeks

Pictured at 4 months

Marty took a Group II at Sunflower Kennel Club Fun Match at three months of age.

Breeder/Owner:	Breeder:
Dananna Dalmatians	Centurion Dalmatians
Jack & Dianna Teeter	Elaine Lindhost
1521 S. 49th St.	49 Oak Springs Ct.
Kansas City, KS 66106-2307	St. Charles, MO 63304
(913) 287-1609	(314) 441-5298